REGENTS RENAISSANCE DRAMA SERIES

General Editor: Cyrus Hoy
Advisory Editor: G. E. Bentley

A MAD WORLD, MY MASTERS

THOMAS MIDDLETON

A Mad World, My Masters

Edited by

STANDISH HENNING

LONDON
EDWARD ARNOLD (PUBLISHERS) LTD.

Printed in Great Britain by
William Clowes and Sons, Limited, London and Beccles

Regents Renaissance Drama Series

The purpose of the Regents Renaissance Drama Series is to provide soundly edited texts, in modern spelling, of the more significant plays of the Elizabethan, Jacobean, and Caroline theater. Each text in the series is based on a fresh collation of all sixteenth- and seventeenth-century editions. The textual notes, which appear above the line at the bottom of each page, record all substantive departures from the edition used as the copy-text. Variant substantive readings among sixteenth- and seventeenth-century editions are listed there as well. In cases where two or more of the old editions present widely divergent readings, a list of substantive variants in editions through the seventeenth century is given in an appendix. Editions after 1700 are referred to in the textual notes only when an emendation originating in some one of them is received into the text. Variants of accidentals (spelling, punctuation, capitalization) are not recorded in the notes. Contracted forms of characters' names are silently expanded in speech prefixes and stage directions, and, in the case of speech prefixes, are regularized. Additions to the stage directions of the copy-text are enclosed in brackets. Stage directions such as "within" or "aside" are enclosed in parentheses when they occur in the copy-text.

Spelling has been modernized along consciously conservative lines. "Murther" has become "murder," and "burthen," "burden," but within the limits of a modernized text, and with the following exceptions, the linguistic quality of the original has been carefully preserved. The variety of contracted forms (*'em, 'am, 'm, 'um, 'hem*) used in the drama of the period for the pronoun *them* are here regularly given as *'em*, and the alternation between *a'th'* and *o'th'* (for *on* or *of the*) is regularly reproduced as *o'th'*. The copy-text distinction between preterite endings in -*d* and -*ed* is preserved except where the elision of *e* occurs in the penultimate syllable; in such cases, the final syllable is contracted. Thus, where the old editions read "threat'ned," those of the present series read "threaten'd." Where, in the old editions, a contracted preterite in -*y'd* would yield -*i'd* in modern spelling (as in "try'd," "cry'd," "deny'd"), the word is here given in its full form (e.g., "tried," "cried," "denied").

Punctuation has been brought into accord with modern practices. The effort here has been to achieve a balance between the generally light pointing of the old editions, and a system of punctuation which, without overloading the text with exclamation marks, semicolons, and dashes, will make the often loosely flowing verse (and prose) of the original syntactically intelligible to the modern reader. Dashes are regularly used only to indicate interrupted speeches, or shifts of address within a single speech.

Explanatory notes, chiefly concerned with glossing obsolete words and phrases, are printed below the textual notes at the bottom of each page. References to stage directions in the notes follow the admirable system of the Revels editions, whereby stage directions are keyed, decimally, to the line of the text before or after which they occur. Thus, a note on 0.2 has reference to the second line of the stage direction at the beginning of the scene in question. A note on 115.1 has reference to the first line of the stage direction following line 115 of the text of the relevant scene.

CYRUS HOY

University of Rochester

Contents

Abbreviations

Barker	Richard Hindry Barker. *Thomas Middleton*. New York, 1958.
Bartholomeus	*Bartholomeus De Proprietatibus Rerum*. London, 1535.
Bullen	A. H. Bullen, ed. *The Works of Thomas Middleton*. 8 vols. London, 1885–1886.
Chambers	Sir Edmund Chambers. *The Elizabethan Stage*. 4 vols. Oxford, 1923.
corr.	corrected.
Dyce	Alexander Dyce, ed. *The Works of Thomas Middleton*. 5 vols. London, 1840.
Eberle	Gerald J. Eberle. *A Critical Edition of Thomas Middleton's A Mad World, My Masters*. Dissertation, University of Wisconsin, 1944.
Linthicum	M. Channing Linthicum. *Costume in the Drama of Shakespeare and his Contemporaries*. Oxford, 1936.
OED	*Oxford English Dictionary*
PBSA	*Publications of the Bibliographical Society of America*
Pliny	*The Historie of the World . . . Translated into English by Philemon Holland*. London, 1601.
Q1	First Quarto of 1608
Q2	Second Quarto of 1640
SB	*Studies in Bibliography*
uncorr.	uncorrected

Introduction

DATE

Thomas Middleton's comedy *A Mad World, My Masters* was entered in the Stationers' Register on October 4, 1608, and was printed before the year was out. The entry is as follows:

Walter Burre Entred for their copie vnder the hand of Master
Eleazer Edgar SEGAR Deputy of Sir GEORGE BUCKE/ and the wardens handes also beinge to yt. A Booke called. *A Mad World (my Maysters)*.

The title page reads in part, "*As it hath bin lately in Action by the Children of Paules*," thus placing *A Mad World* in the repertory of this company of boy actors who flourished in London between 1600 and 1606. Middleton was one of the chief playwrights for the company. The two boys' companies, Paul's and the Children of the Chapel, enjoyed a great vogue in these years, becoming popular enough to make the adult actors anxious for their economic security. They were also involved, through their writers, in the satiric sniping known as the War of the Theaters, the most familiar product of which is the passage in *Hamlet* beginning with Rosencrantz's reference to the "eyrie of children" (II.ii.353 ff.). For unexplained reasons, the Paul's company disappears from all records in the middle of 1606; beginning in May, 1607, a large number of plays from its repertory was entered in the Stationers' Register and subsequently printed, presumably as a last attempt to get money from them.[1]

No precise evidence exists to date the writing of *A Mad World*, though most scholars agree on the years 1604–1606. Follywit's allusion to King James's wholesale knightings which he began on his progress from Edinburgh to London in April and May, 1603, and continued after his coronation in July, marks one chronological limit (I.i.56–59). But the theaters were closed from March 19, 1603, until the next spring owing to the Queen's death and a violent outbreak of the plague;[2] in these months Middleton, like his fellow dramatist

---

[1] Sir Edmund Chambers, *The Elizabethan Stage* (Oxford, 1923), II, 19–23.
[2] *Ibid.*, IV, 335, 336, 349–350.

Dekker, turned to writing pamphlets, probably at the expense of any dramatic work. The cessation of acting by the Children of Paul's sometime after July, 1606, marks the other limit. It seems likely, however, that the play was written after July, 1605. When Mawworm tells Sir Bounteous that the "thieves" have stolen "some hundred pounds in fair spur-royals" from Follywit (II.vi.102), he refers to the ryal or royal, a gold coin minted in the reigns of Mary, Elizabeth, and James, and called a spur-royal because the sunburst on the reverse resembled a spur-rowel. This coin was not minted between 1592 and July, 1605, early in the second minting (1604–1619) of King James.[3] In the decade and more between mintings the Elizabethan royals would have lost a good deal of their glitter and perhaps some of their substance to dishonest men who clipped away their edges. Thus *"fair* spur-royals" are probably freshly minted coins, still unblemished by use or counterfeiters. This supposition seems the more likely as one notices the language of counterfeiting and coining in the play, culminating in the name of Follywit's fake entertainment, *The Slip*, a pun on one term for a counterfeit coin.

THE PLAY

A Mad World belongs to the genre of London, or City, comedies which became so popular at the beginning of the seventeenth century. They are realistic, satiric plays full of the critical force which marks the pamphlets of Green and Nashe and the poems of Marston, Hall, and Donne in the 1590's. Middleton's title catches the tone of this criticism while expressing at the same time the typically detached, ironic attitude found in most of his comedies. More an exclamation than an assertion, "A mad world, my masters," like many folk phrases, indicates an attitude and sounds a warning. By being both amused and exasperated by the *non sequitur* condition of the world, it becomes the verbal counterpart of throwing up the hands. But in the strong word "mad" the phrase recognizes the danger of the world's becoming too intensely or too enduringly unkempt, and so appeals to the hierarchy of values implicit in "masters." The emphasis in this play is on the amusement, for *A Mad World* has less of a palpably moral design on us than most of its contemporaries. As Professor Barker says, Middleton is "ready to tolerate human depravity. He again faces society and again finds it amusing. . . ."[4]

[3] George C. Brooke, *English Coins*, 3rd ed. (London, 1950), pp. 195, 198, 199.

[4] Richard H. Barker, *Thomas Middleton* (New York, 1958), p. 86.

When Penitent Brothel excuses Follywit's roistering as the "common receiv'd riot" of youth, "Time's comic flashes, and the fruits of blood" (I.i.92–93), he identifies for the audience its expected response: Follywit's success is to be measured by the brilliance of his inventive tricks, of which he himself is very proud, rather than by the more sober standards of right and wrong. "Time's comic flashes" is a phrase which urges that no lasting harm can come of the grand larceny just plotted before our eyes, the robbing of his grandfather. Boys will be boys, and the implication is clear that with the passing of time and cooling of the blood, Follywit will become a sensible citizen. Indeed, there is a quality of childish wish-fulfillment in Follywit's rapid, nearly Protean changes of disguise which tend to make him proof against the retaliations of society. From his captaincy in his quasi-military organization of rogues to his transvestite imitation of Frank Gullman he plays so many roles that we scarcely discover who he really is. Next to being invisible, an impenetrable disguise is the best way to free oneself from the prying eye of an adult moral world, and we may wish to see the course of the play as Follywit's last, unsuccessful attempt to hold that world at arm's length. (The same point may be made, with necessary shifts of emphasis, about the other two disguisers, Frank Gullman in her role as virgin, and Penitent Brothel in his brief life as a doctor.) The implicit assurance of Penitent's analysis is in part realized by Follywit's marriage and stated intention to settle down to enjoy his grandfather's substantial wedding gift, and the discovery that he has married his grandfather's whore hardly ruffles him, as it would have if Middleton had wanted this punishment to have didactic significance. There is not even time enough, so close to the end of the play, for Sir Bounteous' scabrous glee over Follywit's misfortune to implant itself in our consciousness ("And since I drink the top, take her; and hark,/ I spice the bottom with a thousand mark," V.ii.263—264). Instead, the revelation of the marriage serves in the play's closing couplet to point what, for lack of a better term, must be called the moral of the play:

> Who lives by cunning, mark it, his fate's cast;
> When he has gull'd all, then is himself the last.

By suppressing Follywit's punishment, Middleton emphasizes the witty, dextrous intrigue which has sped the action along the most violently improbable byways to its slightly soiled conclusion. In doing so he plays essentially the game of Latin comedy where "the ingenuity of [the] devices, the narrowness of the escapes, the success of the execution, not realism, are the tests of excellence."⁵ Jonson, deriving his approach to comedy from the same school, chooses to develop the satiric possibilities more fully and so to invest his plays with an obvious moral indignation. Middleton takes a more sophisticated, ironic line, but one which is also more difficult to control. Follywit's punishment is not severe partly because, in the world of rogues he inhabits, it is both difficult and useless to punish vice and reward virtue. How can any punishment make him fitter than he already is to live in a world with Sir Bounteous, who rewards his grandson's marriage to his own whore with a gift of a thousand marks? Too much wit can lead to folly, but after all it is wit, which as this world goes, deserves its reward—so goes the ironic argument. Sir Bounteous, drowning in his own too-much, has little cause for anger; his grandson has purged him of excess money and married the object of his probably impotent lust,⁶ and he will be a leaner, healthier man for it. (The fact that the burglary is not mentioned at the end shows how little it matters.) Frank Gullman has found her rich husband, and her conventional promise to lead a virtuous life, huddled up into a single couplet, we may believe or not as we choose. With great irony, then, and without comment, Middleton has presented the spectacle of these three enjoying in their own ways the outcome of the plot, and the audience is tacitly invited to assess for itself the validity of their enjoyment.

Yet the habit of didacticism dies hard (perhaps particularly so in one who had paraphrased the *Wisdom of Solomon* before he was twenty), and herein lies the difficulty noted above. Somewhere in most of Middleton's comedies there comes a jarring speech of repentance or remorse, jarring because it suddenly introduces the paraphernalia of standard morality into an action which has been trying to avoid it. The strong moral strain of Penitent's soliloquies attests to a nearly academic desire for a didactic tone, but the isolated nature of the same speeches, separated as they are by the most gleeful attacks on Mistress Harebrain's virtue (and considering the ease with which she deviates from wantonness into virtue), confuses their significance, so that we are left with an impression of earnestness unsupported by credible incident and character. Artistic confusion results from moral

⁵ Madeleine Doran, *Endeavors of Art* (Madison, 1954), p. 153. The chapter on comedy, especially pp. 149–171, is central to this essay.

⁶ Remarks at III.ii.86–88 and V.i.104 hint that Sir Bounteous has not consummated his affair.

uncertainty. If the Penitent-plot were sealed off from the Follywit-plot, the confusion would be less noticeable, but the two plots complement each other in such a way that there is some leakage of the moral tone of one into the other.

In the standard City comedy the hero gulls a rich man out of his money and either marries a creditable girl or seduces a citizen's wife. In *A Mad World*, however, Middleton splits this double aim by giving the seduction to Penitent while marrying Follywit discreditably to the courtesan, the effect of which is to establish the conditions for double actions which may comment ironically upon one another. Both Follywit and Penitent seek dishonest aims, both resort to elaborate schemes involving disguise to achieve their aims, both are successful but with unexpected consequences, and so on. Frank Gullman bridges the two plots in her roles as Sir Bounteous' mistress, Penitent's bawd, and finally Follywit's wife. As a result of this relationship it is difficult for the tone of one line of the action not to affect the tone of the other: Penitent's perfervid, if conventional, morality interferes with the sophisticated coolness with which we are invited to experience Follywit's activity. And it is likely that the leakage is two-way. The immoral delight Penitent and Frank Gullman take in effecting Mistress Harebrain's fall, concentrated in the superb farce of III.ii, is as intense and amusing as Follywit's robbery, and perhaps struck Middleton as too strong to allow for any natural change of heart, leading him to call upon the supernatural succubus to effect Penitent's conversion. Her appearance has often struck critics as a notable breach of the realistic decorum of the play; such objections stem from an unclear notion about the quality of realism in *A Mad World*, but they do record their authors' feelings that somehow Middleton had been forced to stretch too far to make an adequate excuse for that conversion.

It is, rather, the language of his conversion, not the surprising literalness and immediacy of Penitent's vision of hell, that is defective. The characters have been behaving as if there were no moral order in the world for them to contend with, all the while, however, setting in motion forces which will "bring about their own downfall."[7] When Penitent remarks that his appetite for Mistress Harebrain "damns" him (I.i.86), he does not really expect to be taken seriously, but the appearance of the succubus reminds him that damnation

[7] Samuel Schoenbaum, *Middleton's Tragedies* (New York, 1955), p. 168.

need not be a mere metaphor. As for Follywit, for all his acting-directing-producing brilliance, he cannot match Frank Gullman in her role as unblemished maiden. When metaphor becomes reality, and when the trickster is beaten at his own game, a pattern of order emerges which, however ironic, is not cynical. Middleton's amusement is not, I think, to be understood as approval. As Professor Barker says, Middleton "aims to show that sin is blind and that sinners invariably misunderstand the world in which they live, invariably set in motion the forces that bring about their own ruin. The idea is essentially a moral one, even though Middleton works it out without resorting to the crude and obtrusive morality of a Dekker or a Heywood."[8]

Middleton supports his ironic vision with the colloquial tone and movement of his prose. Because it falls midway between the syntactically erratic anti-Ciceronian prose of Jonson and the more symmetrical prose of Shakespeare, it avoids exaggeration in either direction and so maintains a neutral texture. Jonson's sharply satiric tone depends in part upon a syntactic irregularity that characterizes the disordered state of the speakers' minds, as Jonas Barish has shown.[9] Shakespeare's prose, deriving, for all its extraordinary pliability, from the same tradition as Lyly's *Euphues*, is marked by a continuing consecutivity of logic which lends to his characters a high degree of realism.

One finds unsymmetrical syntax most obviously in the speeches of Sir Bounteous where it gives an energetically darting movement to the old man's discourse. More subtly, however, it aids in the portrayal of the egocentrism that lurks behind his delight in hospitality. A typical celebration of that hospitality (II.i.49–58) is marked by the frequent repetition of the personal pronoun "I" separating brief excursions into mock humility: "There's a kind of grace belongs to't, a kind of art which naturally slips from me, I know not on't, I promise you, 'tis gone before I'm aware on't." Miss Ellis-Fermor has wittily noted that Sir Bounteous' charity begins abroad and ends at home,[10] and the asymmetry of the syntax allows him to circle back to himself as frequently as he wishes. In Follywit's speeches, on the other hand, we note a more balanced syntax tending toward parallelism and antithesis, as for example in the early speech where he describes his poverty and intention to rob Sir Bounteous (I.i.33–70). This formality acts in part as a vehicle for the puns and *double-entendres* which are

8 Barker, p. 53.
   Ben Jonson and the Language of Prose Comedy (Cambridge, Mass., 1960).
10 Una Ellis-Fermor, *The Jacobean Drama*, rev. ed. (London, 1958), p. 134

aspects of Follywit's wittiness; the structural similarity of the sentences and of the members within the sentences provides a good context in which the semantic differences of a pun—say the one on "will"—may show themselves. At the same time, the structural regularity gives Follywit's discourse a superficial impression of organization and logic which glosses over his corrupt plan: his unperturbed sureness, which nearly takes the place of motive, puts him in a world where the common distinctions between *mine* and *thine* have no special relevance.

The colloquial middle way, when used in the give and take of conversation, proves to be a fit habitation for the metaphoric language of the play. In *A Mad World* there is none of the iterative imagery which so often forms a special structure of meaning in Shakespeare's plays. Instead, the asymmetrical syntax fosters localized explosions of images, often depending upon puns, such as we find in the first meeting of Penitent and Frank Gullman (I.i.112 ff.). The vocabulary of one art (*wax, wrought, fashioning*) leads to another (*keep time, jar, viol*); when this is completed, the language of finance arises (*business, credit, money*) leading to the puns on the "court of conscience," a small claims court, and on "common place," i.e., the court of common pleas. Yet the dialogue moves so quickly and naturally that we are not conscious of the specific imagery so much as of great energy, for whereas repeated parallel structures draw attention to a pun by providing momentary repose, the realistically erratic conversation, full of movement, draws the attention away from any specific rhetorical device.

Middleton's verse in *A Mad World* is most successful when it carries on the easy colloquial rhythm of the prose. At his best, he writes a very flexible and lucid line which barely echoes the conventional iambic alternation of blank verse and which more often than not exceeds ten syllables. The verse is less effective in the moralizing set pieces, such as that of Penitent at IV.i.1 ff., where it turns stiff and self-conscious, becomes burdened with rhymed *sententiae*, and is hindered by ellipses and other distortions of syntax. It is as if Middleton's esthetic sense were instinctively balking at the forced, contrived morality which has no organic place in his world of rogues, and were instead returning to the inflexible verse of his youthful, dismal *Wisdom of Solomon Paraphrased*. (It may be noted that in the last two speeches of Witgood and the courtesan in *A Trick to Catch the Old One* [1604–1606] Middleton burlesques his moralizing strain.)

The assertion, frequently found in older studies, that Middleton's early comedies are "realistic" can prove troublesome unless one takes pains to discover what is meant. Objections to the appearance of the succubus, noted earlier, seem to be based on a feeling that her supernaturalness contrasts too violently with the tone of the rest of the play, a tone which gives a "spirited transcript of contemporary life," "a faithful and entertaining picture of the life of the time."[11] In fact, as we have seen, the action of *A Mad World*, and to a greater or lesser extent of the other comedies as well, bustles with the improbable activity of fantastic intrigue so that the term "realistic" hardly describes the play. Again, to the extent that these plays isolate a seamy, depraved aspect of the world instead of a noble, romantic one, they are by convention held to be realistic, but such an aspect need not be a "spirited transcript of contemporary life."

Middleton's comedies are full of the scuffle for money; impecunious prodigals prey upon their rich relatives, the relatives in turn are often eager to ruin the young men. Lust for ready cash is complemented by lust for the respectability conferred by the ownership of land, and merchants and decayed gentry circle warily, waiting for the opportunity to pounce. This warfare forms the basic plot of much Jacobean comedy, and if it is realistic in the sense that it reflects the economic unrest of the time,[12] it is too simplified to be a "faithful . . . picture of the life of the time." L. C. Knights has noted the difficulty involved in taking these plays as photographic records of the time when he says: "Reading his comedies as carefully as we can, we find—exciting discovery!—that gallants are likely to be in debt, that they make love to citizens' wives, that lawyers are concerned more for their profits than for justice, and that cut-purses are thieves. Middleton tells us nothing at all about these *as individuals* in a particular place and period."[13] The very sameness of the characters from play to play acts to blur the faithfulness of the picture, leaving us with the impression that the world of these plays is a singularly uncomplicated, if untidy and even nasty place to live. Actually, the sense of realism imparted to us depends principally upon the detail of local color. Topical allusion such as that to the scandalous profusion of King

[11] William Archer, *The Old Drama and the New* (London, 1923), p. 95; E. H. C. Oliphant, *Shakespeare and his Fellow Dramatists* (New York, 1929), II, 10.

[12] See L. C. Knights, *Drama and Society in the Age of Jonson* (London 1951). As Pennyboy Canter cries of Aurelia Clara Pecunia, "Shee is The talke o' the time! th'aduenture o' the Age!" *Staple of News*, I.vi.62–63.

[13] Knights, *Drama and Society*, p. 258.

James's knightings, reference to locales in and around London, glances at feuds in the contemporary acting world—these are the particulars that form a highly recognizable background for the manipulations of the fantastic plot.

In discussing some of the problems of this play I have neglected its riches, but for the most part they resist analysis. *A Mad World, My Masters* is first and last a very funny play, as even the most shocked of the late Victorian critics admitted, and it is notoriously difficult to anatomize the comic. The play revels in obscenity, *double-entendres*, and scatological jokes which I have scarcely ever felt obliged to explicate. Irony at every level of intensity permeates the action and dialogue, and the sheer busy-ness of the multiple disguisings invites Bergsonian analysis. Everyone will have his own favorite scene, but surely Frank Gullman's counterfeit fit, stuffed with every kind of outrageous activity ("farce" comes from the French meaning "stuffed") including the dismissal of those odd allegorical gulls, Inesse and Possibility, will rank at or near the top of all lists. Perhaps we will want to see, in our studies, the obscenity of the play as symptomatic of Follywit's corrupt world, but it is to be doubted whether furrowed brows and pursed lips, often the sign of the student, have any lasting place in the contemplation of this play.

THE TEXT

The first quarto, 1608, is a well-printed play which presents few unusual editorial problems. Printer's copy was doubtless a Middleton holograph, and more than likely the foul papers of the play, that is, an author's draft representing the final version of the substance of the play but containing some ambiguities such as alternative names for characters, descriptive stage directions, unmarked entrances and exits, and the like. Evidence that the printer's copy was in Middleton's hand comes from the appearance in the quarto of certain of his orthographic habits, particularly the odd forms *e'm* for *'em* (*them*), *ha's* for *has*, and the less unusual preterite endings in *-de*.[14] Other evidence points to the foul papers. The stage directions tend to be literary or descriptive of the action beyond the requirements of the stage, a characteristic usually taken to be a sign of the author's hand. Examples such as the following from Act II are typical of the whole

14 See George R. Price, "Setting by Formes in the First Edition of *The Phoenix*," *PBSA*, LVI (1962), 426–427.

play: "*At the other* [*door*], *enter in haste a* Footman"; "*Enter* Follywit *like a lord with his comrades in blue coats*"; "*A strain play'd by the consort,* Sir Bounteous *makes a courtly honor to that lord and seems to foot the tune.*" Such directions would presumably be abbreviated in a prompter's copy derived from the foul papers. Entrances and exits are well marked, the thirty-odd unmarked ones being mostly associated with servants who are called into attendance or sent about their tasks.

Varying character designations, usually strong support in identifying foul papers, appear in a part of the quarto which, because it received peculiar treatment in the printing house, requires additional examination.[15] The first five sheets of the quarto are very well printed, containing no variant readings in the ten known copies, but the rest of the play, sheets F–I, is less satisfactory. In this second section characters who from the first have consistently borne the same name become someone else: Penitent Brothel is Penitent Once-Ill, Harebrain is sometimes Hargrave or Shortrod, and an apparently new character, Semus, appears for the first time. Normally such variation indicates authorial haste or indecision, as in *Romeo and Juliet* where Lady Capulet is designated by a bewildering number of names in the second quarto. Here, however, these variations have been taken as signs of revision either at the time of composition or for a later revival. If the alternate names were the result of Middleton's second thoughts while he was writing the play, they would fall into the category of authorial indecision or haste which marks foul papers. But if they were the result of a later revision, the implication would be that the printer's copy, containing alterations of the original manuscript, would leave signs of the strata of composition.

I find no signs of revision, including that of the names, which cannot be assigned to the work of a careless, inexperienced, or very hurried compositor. His presence is detected at the beginning of sheet F by a change in the spelling of the speech designations and by a large number of misreadings. The absence of variants in the first five sheets argues that the two compositors who set the first section were able workmen who found their copy easy to deal with; but the second section is full of variants, sheet H, for example, existing in three states of progressive amendment. The compositor of this

15 See Gerald J. Eberle, "The Composition and Printing of Middleton's *A Mad World, My Masters,*" *SB*, III (1950), 246–252. I am grateful to Professor Eberle for personal kindnesses given during the preparation of this edition.

section produces "Gilfer" for "Pilfer," "Niter" for "Miter," "seard" for "seazd"; he omits a stage direction; he sets "fare him well" for the undoubted "fare thee well," and makes a number of other errors in pronouns. If it were not for the egregious literal errors it might be supposed that the printer's manuscript were radically different after sheet E, becoming much harder to read and to interpret, but this compositor's incompetence is manifest. It thus seems likely that the variations in the characters' names result from his inability to cope with a moderately ambiguous manuscript. The better compositors apparently found it possible to regularize whatever variations they found, but were unable to instruct their successor when he began working. Their work invites confidence, and their reading of *Gunwater* instead of *Gumwater* has been adopted.

Finally, the compositors set the play by casting off copy, that is, dividing the manuscript into sections equal to a page of type. The advantage of this technique is that the press, which prints pages one, four, five, and eight of a quarto on one side of a sheet, can be put to work faster than if the compositor sets the manuscript page by page. The difficulty in using this technique is that when, as occasionally happens, miscalculation of the manuscript allots too many or too few lines for the type page, the compositor must adjust his copy as best he can, and this may lead to his treating prose as verse and verse as prose, to placing two speeches on a line, to an unusually frequent use of the tilde and ampersand to contract words, and even in extreme cases to leaving out what simply cannot be squeezed in. The editor's task is made easier when he knows that the method has been employed, since he obtains additional insight into the nature of the printer's copy.

The second quarto, 1640, is a reprint of Q1 which corrects some of the obvious mistakes and makes a considerable number of its own. Fortunately, it was printed from a copy of Q1 bearing the corrected sheets. The title page says that the play "hath bin often Acted at the Private House in *Salisbury Court*, by her Majesties Servants." This company, Queen Henrietta's, has a history extending from 1625 to 1642; it was a reorganized group, however, that played at Salisbury Court between 1637 and 1642, and it is to this group that the revival belongs.[16] The additional stage directions at the end of acts two and five seem to point to some minor refurbishing for the Salisbury Court

16 G. E. Bentley, *The Jacobean and Caroline Stage* (Oxford, 1941–1956), I, 218–259.

performances. Whether the song printed at the end of the quarto under the title *Catch for the Fifth Act* was in fact performed, or simply added by the printer to fill an empty page, is not clear, nor is it important. Bullen notes that the song "is printed in Lyly's *Alexander and Campaspe*, i.2,—in Blount's edition of 1632, not in earlier eds. Perhaps neither Middleton nor Lyly wrote it."

A Mad World, My Masters was reprinted five times in the eighteenth and nineteenth centuries: in Robert Dodsley's *Select Collection of Old Plays*, second edition, 1780; in *Ancient British Drama*, 1810, edited by Sir Walter Scott; in the third edition of Dodsley's *Plays*, 1825–1827, edited by J. Payne Collier; and in the two collected *Works of Thomas Middleton*, edited by Alexander Dyce (1840) and A. H. Bullen (1885–1886). By an odd irony, all the editions but Collier's are derived from a copy or copies of the first quarto bearing uncorrected sheets, some readings being corrected by recourse to Q2. Dyce, whose own copy has the uncorrected sheets, rejects a number of correct Q2 readings. Nevertheless, his edition is the most important of the five because it provides a collection of good notes and identifies a considerable amount of verse hidden in the prose lines. If modern editorial practice does not accept all of Dyce's arrangements, it is still in his debt for having worked so well on the text of Middleton. For the sake of convenience and brevity in the notes, I have credited Dyce alone for explanations when he has himself credited earlier editors.

STANDISH HENNING

University of Wisconsin

NOTE. Since completing this edition, I have discovered that the problematic sheets F–I were printed in the shop of Nicholas Okes, not in that of Henry Ballard as the title page seems to suggest. This discovery helps to account for the anomalies noted on pages xviii and xix, above.

A MAD WORLD, MY MASTERS

The Actors in the Comedy

SIR BOUNTEOUS PROGRESS	*an old rich knight*	
RICHARD FOLLYWIT	*nephew to Sir Bounteous Progress*	
MASTER PENITENT BROTHEL	*a country gentleman*	
MAWWORM, a lieutenant ⎫		5
HOBOY, an ancient ⎭	*comrades to Follywit*	
MASTER INESSE ⎫		
MASTER POSSIBILITY ⎭	*two [elder] brothers*	10
MASTER HAREBRAIN	*a citizen*	
GUNWATER	*Sir Bounteous' man*	
JASPER	*Penitent's man*	
RALPH	*Master Harebrain's man*	
TWO KNIGHTS		15
ONE CONSTABLE		
A SUCCUBUS		
WATCHMEN		
A FOOTMAN		
AN OLD GENTLEWOMAN	*mother to the courtesan*	20
MISTRESS HAREBRAIN	*the citizen's wife*	
FRANK GULLMAN	*the courtesan*	
ATTENDANTS		

1.] Adapted from *Q2.*

7. *Hoboy*] a variant of hautboy, oboe. Q2 prints *Hobby*, i.e., hobbyhorse.

7. *ancient*] ensign.

8, 10.] "Inesse and Possibility are . . . two names [that] must be read together. An estate *in esse* (in being) gave possession of land; an estate in possibility would give possession after the estate *in esse* ended" (William Power, "Middleton's Way with Names," *Notes and Queries*, N.S., VII [April, 1960], 139). The point is that they are rich.

22. *Frank*] a diminutive of Frances.

A Mad World, My Masters

[I.i]

Enter Dick Follywit, *and his consorts*, Lieutenant Mawworm, Ancient Hoboy, *and others his comrades.*

MAWWORM.

    Oh, captain, regent, principal!

HOBOY.

    What shall I call thee? The noble spark of bounty, the lifeblood of society!

FOLLYWIT.

    Call me your forecast, you whoresons. When you come drunk out of a tavern, 'tis I must cast your plots into form 5
still; 'tis I must manage the prank, or I'll not give a louse for the proceeding; I must let fly my civil fortunes, turn wild-brain, lay my wits upo'th' tenters, you rascals, to maintain a company of villains whom I love in my very soul and conscience. 10

MAWWORM.

    Aha, our little forecast!

FOLLYWIT.

    Hang you, you have bewitch'd me among you. I was as well given till I fell to be wicked, my grandsire had hope of me, I went all in black, swore but o' Sundays, never came home drunk but upon fasting nights to cleanse my stomach; 'slid, 15
now I'm quite altered, blown into light colors, let out oaths by th' minute, sit up late till it be early, drink drunk till I am sober, sink down dead in a tavern and rise in a tobacco shop. Here's a transformation. I was wont yet to pity the

---

6. *still*] always.
8. *tenters*] a frame for stretching cloth.
12–22.] Editors have noted the parody of Falstaff's speech, *1 Henry IV*, III.iii.15–23.

simple, and leave 'em some money; 'slid, now I gull 'em   20
without conscience. I go without order, swear without
number, gull without mercy, and drink without measure.

MAWWORM.

I deny the last, for if you drink ne'er so much, you drink
within measure.

FOLLYWIT.

How prove you that, sir?   25

MAWWORM.

Because the drawers never fill their pots.

FOLLYWIT.

Mass, that was well found out; all drunkards may lawfully
say they drink within measure by that trick. And, now I'm
put i'th' mind of a trick, can you keep your countenance,
villains? Yet I am a fool to ask that, for how can they keep   30
their countenance that have lost their credits?

HOBOY.

I warrant you for blushing, captain.

FOLLYWIT.

I easily believe that, ancient, for thou lost thy colors once.
Nay, faith, as for blushing, I think there's grace little enough
amongst you all; 'tis Lent in your cheeks, the flag's down.   35
Well, your blushing face I suspect not, nor indeed greatly
your laughing face, unless you had more money in your
purses. Then thus compendiously, now. You all know the
possibilities of my hereafter fortunes, and the humor of my
frolic grandsire, Sir Bounteous Progress, whose death makes   40
all possible to me: I shall have all when he has nothing; but
now he has all, I shall have nothing. I think one mind runs
through a million of 'em; they love to keep us sober all the
while they're alive, that when they're dead we may drink
to their healths; they cannot abide to see us merry all the   45

29. can you] *Q1*; you can *Q2*.   40. death makes] *Q1*; deaths make
33. thou lost] *Q1*; thou hast lost *Q2*.   *Q2*.

---

29. *countenance*] repute, with a pun on "financial credit."

33. *lost . . . colors*] an ancient (ensign) was a flag bearer; to lose the flag
to the enemy was a great shame.

35. *Lent . . . down*] Flags flown from the playhouses during performances
were taken down when acting was prohibited, as during Lent.

39. *humor*] whim.

while they're above ground, and that makes so many laugh
at their fathers' funerals. I know my grandsire has his will
in a box, and has bequeath'd all to me when he can carry
nothing away; but stood I in need of poor ten pounds now,
by his will I should hang myself ere I should get it. There's   50
no such word in his will, I warrant you, nor no such thought
in his mind.

MAWWORM.

You may build upon that, captain.

FOLLYWIT.

Then, since he has no will to do me good as long as he lives,
by mine own will I'll do myself good before he dies. And   55
now I arrive at the purpose. You are not ignorant, I'm sure,
you true and necessary implements of mischief, first, that my
grandsire Sir Bounteous Progress is a knight of thousands,
and therefore no knight since one thousand six hundred;
next, that he keeps a house like his name, bounteous, open   60
for all comers; thirdly and lastly, that he stands much upon
the glory of his complement, variety of entertainment,
together with the largeness of his kitchen, longitude of his
buttery, and fecundity of his larder, and thinks himself
never happier than when some stiff lord or great countess   65
alights to make light his dishes. These being well mix'd together may give my project better encouragement, and
make my purpose spring forth more fortunate. To be short,
and cut off a great deal of dirty way, I'll down to my
grandsire like a lord.   70

MAWWORM.

How, captain?

FOLLYWIT.

A French ruff, a thin beard, and a strong perfume will do't.
I can hire blue coats for you all by Westminster clock, and

54. no will] *Q1*; no good will *Q2*.

---

59. *no . . . hundred*] In 1603 James I required that all landholders worth
forty pounds a year be knighted or else suffer a fine.

72. *French ruff*] "a deep ruff, which, instead of extending at right angles
to the neck, hung down from the top of a high stock which was fastened up
to the chin" (Linthicum, p. 160).

73. *blue coats*] the dress of servants. Why they should be available near
Westminster clock is not clear.

that color will be soonest believed.

MAWWORM.

But prithee, captain—   75

FOLLYWIT.

Push, I reach past your fathoms: you desire crowns.

MAWWORM.

From the crown of our head to the sole of our foot, bully.

FOLLYWIT.

Why, carry yourselves but probably, and carry away
enough with yourselves.

Enter Master Penitent Brothel.

HOBOY.

Why, there spoke a Roman captain. Master Penitent   80
Brothel—

PENITENT.

Sweet Master Follywit—

Exeunt [*all but* Penitent Brothel].
Here's a mad-brain o'th' first, whose pranks scorn to have
precedents, to be second to any, or walk beneath any mad-
cap's inventions; h'as play'd more tricks than the cards can   85
allow a man, and of the last stamp, too; hating imitation,
a fellow whose only glory is to be prime of the company, to
be sure of which he maintains all the rest.
He's the carrion, and they the kites that gorge upon him.
But why in others do I check wild passions,   90
And retain deadly follies in myself?
I tax his youth of common receiv'd riot,
Time's comic flashes, and the fruits of blood;
And in myself soothe up adulterous motions,
And such an appetite that I know damns me,   95
Yet willingly embrace it: love to Harebrain's wife,
Over whose hours and pleasures her sick husband,
With a fantastic but deserv'd suspect,

82.1. *Exeunt*] *Dyce*; *Exit Q1.*

76. *fathoms*] hints, gropings.
76. *crowns*] coins.
83. *o'th' first*] in heraldry, the color first mentioned in blazoning a coat of
arms; here, a superlative.
86. *last stamp*] most recent mintage.

Bestows his serious time in watch and ward.
And therefore I'm constrain'd to use the means   100
Of one that knows no mean, a courtesan,
One poison for another, whom her husband
Without suspicion innocently admits
Into her company, who with tried art
Corrupts and loosens her most constant powers,   105
Making his jealousy more than half a wittol,
Before his face plotting his own abuse,
To which himself gives aim,

Enter Courtesan.

Whilst the broad arrow with the forked head
Misses his brow but narrowly. See, here she comes,   110
The close courtesan, whose mother is her bawd.

COURTESAN.

Master Penitent Brothel!

PENITENT.

My little pretty Lady Gullman, the news, the comfort?

COURTESAN.

Y'are the fortunate man, Sir Knight o'th' Holland Shirt.
There wants but opportunity and she's wax of your own   115
fashioning. She had wrought herself into the form of your
love before my art set finger to her.

PENITENT.

Did our affections meet, our thoughts keep time?

COURTESAN.

So it should seem by the music. The only jar is in the
grumbling bass viol, her husband.   120

PENITENT.

Oh, his waking suspicion!

COURTESAN.

Sigh not, Master Penitent, trust the managing of the business with me; 'tis for my credit now to see't well finish'd.
If I do you no good, sir, you shall give me no money, sir.

---

112. Brothel] *Q1*; *Brothwell Q2.*   114. Shirt] *Dyce*; skirt *Q1-2.*

106. *wittol*] contented cuckold.
108. *To . . . aim*] which he directs. In archery, a man standing near the
targets gives aim when he reports the accuracy of the shot.
111. *close*] secret.

PENITENT.

I am arriv'd at the court of conscience! A courtesan! Oh 125
admirable times! Honesty is removed to the common place.
Farewell, lady.   *Exit* Penitent.

Enter Mother.

MOTHER.

How now, daughter?

COURTESAN.

What news, mother?

MOTHER.

A token from thy keeper.   130

COURTESAN.

Oh, from Sir Bounteous Progress. He's my keeper indeed,
but there's many a piece of venison stol'n that my keeper
wots not on; there's no park kept so warily but loses flesh
one time or other, and no woman kept so privately but may
watch advantage to make the best of her pleasure. And in 135
common reason one keeper cannot be enough for so proud a
park as a woman.

MOTHER.

Hold thee there, girl.

COURTESAN.

Fear not me, mother.

MOTHER.

Every part of the world shoots up daily into more subtlety. 140
The very spider weaves her cauls with more art and cunning
to entrap the fly.
The shallow plowman can distinguish now
'Twixt simple truth and a dissembling brow,
Your base mechanic fellow can spy out   145
A weakness in a lord, and learns to flout.
How does't behoove us then that live by sleight

---

125. *court of conscience*] Court of Requests, a popular and just small claims
court established in 1517 and reconfirmed by act of parliament in 1603.

126. *common place*] "A pun, I presume,—common-pleas" (Dyce), i.e., one
of the three major courts of law.

133. *wots not on*] does not know about.

141. *cauls*] spider webs.

145. *mechanic*] laboring.

To have our wits wound up to their stretch'd height!
Fifteen times thou know'st I have sold thy maidenhead
To make up a dowry for thy marriage, and yet   150
There's maidenhead enough for old Sir Bounteous still.
He'll be all his lifetime about it yet,
And be as far to seek when he has done.
The sums that I have told upon thy pillow!
I shall once see those golden days again;   155
Though fifteen, all thy maidenheads are not gone.
The Italian is not serv'd yet, nor the French;
The British men come for a dozen at once,
They engross all the market. Tut, my girl,
'Tis nothing but a politic conveyance,   160
A sincere carriage, a religious eyebrow
That throws their charms over the worldings' senses;
And when thou spiest a fool that truly pities
The false springs of thine eyes,
And honorably dotes upon thy love,   165
If he be rich, set him by for a husband.
Be wisely tempered and learn this, my wench,
Who gets th' opinion for a virtuous name
May sin at pleasure, and ne'er think of shame.

COURTESAN.
Mother, I am too deep a scholar grown   170
To learn my first rules now.

MOTHER.   'Twill be thy own,
I say no more. Peace, hark. Remove thyself.   [*Exit* Courtesan.]
Oh, the two elder brothers.

                Enter Inesse *and* Possibility.

POSSIBILITY.
A fair hour, sweet lady.

MOTHER.
Good morrow, gentlemen, Master Inesse and Master 175
Possibility.

INESSE.
Where's the little sweet lady your daughter?

152–153.] *Dyce; prose in Q1–2.*   171. thy] *Q1;* thine *Q2.*

160. *conveyance*] behavior, with a sense of "cunning, trickery."
168. *opinion*] reputation.

MOTHER.

    Even at her book, sir.

POSSIBILITY.

    So religious?

MOTHER.

    'Tis no new motion, sir; sh'as took it from an infant.   180

POSSIBILITY.

    May we deserve a sight of her, lady?

MOTHER.

    Upon that condition you will promise me, gentlemen, to
    avoid all profane talk, wanton compliments, undecent
    phrases, and lascivious courtings, which I know my
    daughter will sooner die than endure, I am contented your 185
    suits shall be granted.

POSSIBILITY.

    Not a bawdy syllable, I protest.

INESSE.

    Syllable was well-plac'd there, for indeed your one syllables
    are your bawdiest words: prick that down.   *Exeunt.*

[I.ii]   *Enter* Master Harebrain.

HAREBRAIN.

    She may make nightwork on't; 'twas well recovered. He-
    cats and courtesans stroll most i'th' night; her friend may be
    receiv'd and convey'd forth nightly. I'll be at charge for
    watch and ward, for watch and ward, i' faith; and here
    they come.   5

            Enter two or three [Watchmen].

FIRST WATCHMAN.

    Give your worship good even.

HAREBRAIN.

    Welcome, my friends; I must deserve your diligence in an

---

181. May we] *Q1*; We may *Q2*.   couered/ Hee...night/ Her...
188. well-plac'd] *Dyce*; plac'st *Q1–2*.   nightly *Q1–2*.
[I.ii]   5.1. Watchmen] *Q2*; *not in Q1*.
1–3. She . . . nightly] She . . . re-

    1. *recovered*] outwitted (?). Dyce suggests "discovered," referring to line
9 below.

employment serious. The truth is, there is a cunning plot laid,
but happily discovered, to rob my house; the night un-
certain when, but fix'd within the circle of this month. 10
Nor does this villainy consist in numbers,
Or many partners; only someone
Shall, in the form of my familiar friend,
Be receiv'd privately into my house
By some perfidious servant of mine own,   15
Address'd fit for the practice.

FIRST WATCHMAN.   Oh, abominable!

HAREBRAIN.

If you be faithful watchmen, show your goodness,
And with these angels shore up your eyelids.
Let me not be purloin'd—[*aside*] purloin'd indeed; the merry
Greeks conceive me. —There is a gem I would not lose, 20
kept by the Italian under lock and key; we Englishmen are
careless creatures. Well, I have said enough.

SECOND WATCHMAN.

And we will do enough, sir.   *Exeunt* [Watchmen].

HAREBRAIN.

Why, well said, watch me a good turn now; so, so, so.
Rise villainy with the lark, why 'tis prevented,   25
Or steal't by with the leather-winged bat,
The evening cannot save it. Peace—

[*Enter* Courtesan.]

Oh, Lady Gullman, my wife's only company, welcome! And
how does the virtuous matron, that good old gentlewoman
thy mother? I persuade myself if modesty be in the world 30

---

16. *Address'd . . . practice*] prepared for the trick.
18. *angels*] gold coins worth about ten shillings stamped with the figure
of St. Michael killing a dragon.
19. *purloin'd*] Eberle suggests an elaborate pun: "pur," the knave in a
card game called post and pair; "loin," to copulate. Thus, loined by a
knave.
19–20. *merry Greeks*] sly, tricky fellows.
21. *kept . . . key*] Bullen quotes Burton's *Anatomy of Melancholy*, III.iii.1.2:
"The Italians 'lock up their women, and will not suffer them to be near
men so much as in the church, but with a partition between.'"
25. *prevented*] frustrated.

she has part on't. A woman of an excellent carriage all her
lifetime, in court, city, and country.

COURTESAN.

Sh'as always carried it well in those places, sir. —[*Aside.*]
Witness three bastards apiece. —How does your sweet bed-
fellow, sir? You see I'm her boldest visitant.   35

HAREBRAIN.

And welcome, sweet virgin, the only companion my soul
wishes for her. I left her within at her lute; prithee give her
good counsel.

COURTESAN.

Alas, she needs none, sir.

HAREBRAIN.

Yet, yet, yet, a little of thy instructions will not come amiss   40
to her.

COURTESAN.

I'll bestow my labor, sir.

HAREBRAIN.

Do, labor her, prithee; I have convey'd away all her
wanton pamphlets, as *Hero and Leander, Venus and Adonis*; oh,
two luscious mary-bone pies for a young married wife. Here,   45
here, prithee take the *Resolution*, and read to her a little.

COURTESAN.

Sh'as set up her resolution already, sir.

HAREBRAIN.

True, true, and this will confirm it the more. There's a
chapter of hell 'tis good to read this cold weather. Terrify
her, terrify her; go, read to her the horrible punishments for   50
itching wantonness, the pains allotted for adultery; tell her
her thoughts, her very dreams are answerable; say so, rip
up the life of a courtesan, and show how loathsome 'tis.

COURTESAN [*aside*].

The gentleman would persuade me in time to disgrace

---

44. *Hero . . . Adonis*] Marlowe's and Shakespeare's Ovidian poems.
45. *mary-bone*] marrow bone, an aphrodisiac.
46. *Resolution*] *The First Book of the Christian Exercise Pertaining to Resolution*
(1582), a very popular book of devotion written by the Jesuit Robert
Parsons.

myself, and speak ill of mine own function.   *Exit.*   55

HAREBRAIN.

    This is the course I take. I'll teach the married man

    A new selected strain. I admit none

    But this pure virgin to her company;

    Puh, that's enough. I'll keep her to her stint,

    I'll put her to her pension;   60

    She gets but her allowance, that's a bare one;

    Few women but have that beside their own.

    Ha, ha, ha, nay, I'll put her hard to't.

       Enter wife [Mistress Harebrain] *and* Courtesan.

MISTRESS HAREBRAIN.

    Fain would I meet the gentleman.

COURTESAN.

    Push, fain would you meet him! Why, you do not take the   65

    course.

HAREBRAIN.

    How earnestly she labors her, like a good wholesome sister

    of the Family. She will prevail, I hope.

COURTESAN.

    Is that the means?

MISTRESS HAREBRAIN.

    What is the means? I would as gladly to enjoy his sight,   70

    embrace it as the—

COURTESAN.

    Shall I have hearing? Listen—

HAREBRAIN.

    She's round with her, i' faith.

COURTESAN.

    When husbands in their rank'st suspicions dwell,

    Then 'tis our best art to dissemble well.   75

    Put but these notes in use that I'll direct you,

    He'll curse himself that e'er he did suspect you.

    Perhaps he will solicit you, as in trial,

---

61. a] *Dyce; not in Q 1–2.*

---

  68. *Family*] the Family of Love, a religious sect which held that religion consisted chiefly in the exercise of love. Middleton, Jonson and others use the Family to attack sexual hypocrisy.

To visit such and such: still give denial.
Let no persuasions sway you; they are but fetches   80
Set to betray you, jealousies, slights, and reaches.
Seem in his sight to endure the sight of no man;
Put by all kisses, till you kiss in common;
Neglect all entertain; if he bring in
Strangers, keep you your chamber, be not seen;   85
If he chance steal upon you, let him find
Some book lie open 'gainst an unchaste mind,
And coted scriptures, though for your own pleasure
You read some stirring pamphlet, and convey it
Under your skirt, the fittest place to lay it.   90
This is the course, my wench, to enjoy thy wishes;
Here you perform best when you most neglect;
The way to daunt is to outvie suspect.
Manage these principles but with art and life,
Welcome all nations, thou'rt an honest wife.   95

HAREBRAIN.

She puts it home, i' faith, ev'n to the quick.
From her elaborate action I reach that
I must requite this maid. Faith, I'm forgetful. [*Draws back.*]

MISTRESS HAREBRAIN.

Here, lady,
Convey my heart unto him in this jewel.   100
Against you see me next you shall perceive
I have profited. In the mean season, tell him
I am a prisoner yet, o'th' master's side.
My husband's jealousy,
That masters him as he doth master me,   105
And as a keeper that locks prisoners up
Is himself prison'd under his own key,
Even so my husband, in restraining me,
With the same ward bars his own liberty.

84. entertain] *Q1*; entertainment   104–105.] *Dyce; one line in Q1–2.*
Q2.

---

88. *coted*] quoted.   93. *suspect*] suspicion.   101. *Against*] when.
103. *master's side*] "The governor of a prison was allowed to let certain
rooms for his own profit; hence 'to lie on the master's side' meant to have
the best lodging in the prison" (Bullen).

COURTESAN.

    I'll tell him how you wish it, and I'll wear   110
    My wits to the third pile, but all shall clear.

MISTRESS HAREBRAIN.

    I owe you more than thanks, but that I hope
    My husband will requite you.

COURTESAN.

    Think you so, lady? He has small reason for't.

HAREBRAIN.

    What, done so soon? Away, to't again, to't again, good 115
    wench to't again; leave her not so. Where left you? Come—

COURTESAN.

    Faith, I am weary, sir.
    I cannot draw her from her strict opinion
    With all the arguments that sense can frame.

HAREBRAIN.

    No? Let me come. Fie, wife, you must consent; what 120
    opinion is't, let's hear?

COURTESAN.

    Fondly and willfully she retains that thought
    That every sin is damn'd.

HAREBRAIN.

    Oh, fie, fie, wife! Pea, pea, pea, pea, how have you lost your
    time? For shame, be converted. There's a diabolical 125
    opinion indeed. Then you may think that usury were
    damn'd; you're a fine merchant, i' faith. Or bribery? you
    know the law well. Or sloth? would some of the clergy
    heard you, i' faith. Or pride? you come at court. Or
    gluttony? you're not worthy to dine at an alderman's table. 130
    Your only deadly sin's adultery,
    That villainous ringworm, woman's worst requital.
    'Tis only lechery that's damn'd to th' pit-hole;

110. wish] *Q1*; wisht *Q2*.   126. Then] *Q1*; That *Q2*.
112. thanks] *Q1*; thanke *Q2*.

---

    111. *third pile*] probably the satin ground above which two piles were
formed to make rich velvet (see Linthicum, p. 126).
    119. *sense*] intellectual power, but with an oblique reference to sensuality.
    122. *Fondly*] foolishly.
    132. *requital*] repayment, but ironically also "revenge."

Ah, that's an arch-offence; believe it, squall,
All sins are venial but venereal.   135

COURTESAN.

I've said enough to her.

HAREBRAIN.

And she will be rul'd by you.

COURTESAN.

Fah!

HAREBRAIN.

I'll pawn my credit on't. Come hither, lady,
I will not altogether rest ingrateful;   140
Here, wear this ruby for thy pains and counsel.

COURTESAN.

It is not so much worth, sir. I am a very ill counselor, truly.

HAREBRAIN.

Go to, I say.

COURTESAN.

Y'are too blame, i' faith, sir; I shall ne'er deserve it.

HAREBRAIN.

Thou hast done't already. Farewell, sweet virgin, prithee 145
let's see thee oft'ner.

COURTESAN [aside].

Such gifts will soon entreat me.   *Exit.*

HAREBRAIN.

Wife, as thou lov'st the quiet of my breast,
Embrace her counsel, yield to her advices;
Thou wilt find comfort in 'em in the end,   150
Thou'lt feel an alteration; prithee think on't.
Mine eyes can scarce refrain.

MISTRESS HAREBRAIN.

Keep in your dew, sir, lest when you would, you want it.

HAREBRAIN.

I've pawn'd my credit on't. Ah, didst thou know
The sweet fruit once, thou'dst never let it go.   155

---

135. sins] *Q1*; sinners *Q2*.   155. thou'dst] *Q1*; thou'lst *Q2*.

---

134. *squall*] a term of endearment.
144. *too blame*] "In the 16–17th c. the *to* was [often] misunderstood as *too*,
and blame was taken as adj. blameworthy, culpable" (*OED*).

MISTRESS HAREBRAIN.
 'Tis that I strive to get.

HAREBRAIN.   And still do so.   *Exeunt.*

                      Finit Actus Primus.

[II.i]   *Incipit Actus Secundus.*
                Enter Sir Bounteous *with two* Knights.

FIRST KNIGHT.
 You have been too much like your name, Sir Bounteous.

SIR BOUNTEOUS.
 Oh, not so, good knights, not so, you know my humor; most
 welcome, good Sir Andrew Polcut, Sir Aquitaine Colewort,
 most welcome.

BOTH.
 Thanks, good Sir Bounteous.   *Exeunt at one door.*   5

           At the other, enter in haste a Footman.

FOOTMAN.
 Oh, cry your worship heartily mercy, sir.

SIR BOUNTEOUS.
 How now, linen stockings and threescore-mile-a-day,
 whose footman art thou?

FOOTMAN.
 Pray can your worship tell me—[*panting*] hoh, hoh, hoh—if
 my lord be come in yet?   10

SIR BOUNTEOUS.
 Thy lord! What lord?

FOOTMAN.
 My Lord Owemuch, sir.

SIR BOUNTEOUS.
 My Lord Owemuch! I have heard much speech of that
 lord; h'as great acquaintance i'th' city. That lord has been
 much followed.   15

156.1. *Finit*] *Q1*; *Finis Q2.*   3. Andrew Polcut] *Q2*; Andro
[II.i]   Pelcut *Q1.*
2. knights] *Q1*; Knight *Q2.*

---

 14. *city*] then as now the financial center of the larger metropolis.

FOOTMAN.

And is still, sir; he wants no company when he's in London.
He's free of the mercers, and there's none of 'em all dare
cross him.

SIR BOUNTEOUS.

And they did, he'd turn over a new leaf with 'em; he would
make 'em all weary on't i'th' end. Much fine rumor have I   20
heard of that lord, yet had I never the fortune to set eye
upon him. Art sure he will alight here, footman? I am afraid
thou'rt mistook.

FOOTMAN.

Thinks your worship so, sir? By your leave, sir.

SIR BOUNTEOUS.

Puh! Passion of me, footman! Why, pumps, I say come back!   25

FOOTMAN.

Does your worship call?

SIR BOUNTEOUS.

Come hither, I say. I am but afraid on't; would it might
happen so well. How dost know? Did he name the house
with the great turret o'th' top?

FOOTMAN.

No, faith, did he not, sir.   30

SIR BOUNTEOUS.

Come hither, I say. Did he speak of a cloth o' gold chamber?

FOOTMAN.

Not one word, by my troth, sir.

SIR BOUNTEOUS.

Come again, you lousy seven-mile-an-hour.

FOOTMAN.

I beseech your worship, detain me not.

SIR BOUNTEOUS.

Was there no talk of a fair pair of organs, a great gilt   35
candlestick, and a pair of silver snuffers?

---

17. *free . . . mercers*] an honorary member of the cloth-sellers guild.
"*The mercer's book*: proverbial in the Elizabethan period with reference to
the debts of a gallant" (*OED*).

19. *And*] if; frequently used and not hereafter glossed.

25. *pumps*] i.e., the footman, who wore pumps.

35. *pair . . . organs*] old term for organ.

FOOTMAN.

'Twere sin to belie my lord; I heard no such words, sir.

SIR BOUNTEOUS.

A pox confine thee, come again! Puh!

FOOTMAN.

Your worship will undo me, sir.

SIR BOUNTEOUS.

Was there no speech of a long dining room, a huge kitchen, 40
large meat, and a broad dresser board?

FOOTMAN.

I have a greater maw to that, indeed, an't please your
worship.

SIR BOUNTEOUS.

Whom did he name?

FOOTMAN.

Why, one Sir Bounteous Progress. 45

SIR BOUNTEOUS.

Ah, a, a, I am that Sir Bounteous, you progressive round-
about rascal!

FOOTMAN (*laughs*).

Puh!

SIR BOUNTEOUS.

I knew I should have him i'th' end; there's not a lord will
miss me, I thank their good honors; 'tis a fortune laid upon 50
me, they can scent out their best entertainment; I have a
kind of complimental gift given me above ordinary country
knights, and how soon 'tis smelt out! I warrant ye there's not
one knight i'th' shire able to entertain a lord i'th' cue, or a
lady i'th' nick like me, like me. There's a kind of grace 55
belongs to't, a kind of art which naturally slips from me, I
know not on't, I promise you, 'tis gone before I'm aware
on't. Cuds me, I forget myself. Where!

[*Enter* Servants.]

FIRST SERVANT.

Does your worship call?

48. S. D. *laughs*] *set as part of Foot-*   51. out] *Q1*; *our Q2*.
man's speech in Q1.

41. *dresser board*] a table on which food was prepared.

SIR BOUNTEOUS.

Run, sirrah, call in my chief gentleman i'th' chain of gold,   60
expedite. [*Exit* First Servant.] And how does my good lord?
I never saw him before in my life. —A cup of bastard for this
footman.

FOOTMAN.

My lord has travel'd this five year, sir.

SIR BOUNTEOUS.

Travail'd this five year? How many children has he? —Some   65
bastard, I say!

FOOTMAN.

No bastard, an't please your worship.

SIR BOUNTEOUS.

A cup of sack to strengthen his wit. [*Exit* Second Servant.]
The footman's a fool.

[*Enter* Gunwater.]

Oh, come hither, Master Gunwater, come hither. Send   70
presently to Master Pheasant for one of his hens; there's
partridge i'th' house.

GUNWATER.

And wild duck, an't please your worship.

SIR BOUNTEOUS.

And woodcock, an't please thy worship.

GUNWATER.

And woodcock, an't please your worship. I had thought to   75
have spoke before you.

SIR BOUNTEOUS.

Remember the pheasant, down with some plover, clap down
six woodcocks: my lord's coming. Now, sir?

GUNWATER.

An't please your worship, there's a lord and his followers
newly alighted.   80

75. woodcock] *Q1*; woodcocks *Q2*.   78. lord's] *Dyce*; loue's *Q1-2*.

---

60. *chain . . . gold*] insignia worn by stewards.
62. *bastard*] sweet Spanish wine.
64–65. *travel'd . . . Travail'd*] a common pun on "travel" and the "labor
of childbirth."
68. *sack*] sweet white wine.

SIR BOUNTEOUS.

    Dispatch, I say, dispatch! Why, where's my music? He's
come indeed.

    Enter Follywit *like a lord with his comrades in blue coats.*

FOLLYWIT.

    Footman.

FOOTMAN.

    My lord?

FOLLYWIT.

    Run swiftly with my commendations to Sir Jasper Topaz;   85
we'll ride and visit him i'th' morning, say.

FOOTMAN.

    Your lordship's charge shall be effected.   *Exit.*

FOLLYWIT.

    That courtly, comely form should present to me Sir Bounte-
ous Progress.

SIR BOUNTEOUS.

    Y'ave found me out, my lord; I cannot hide myself. Your   90
honor is most spaciously welcome.

FOLLYWIT.

    In this forgive me, sir,
That being a stranger to your houses and you,
I make my way so bold, and presume
Rather upon your kindness than your knowledge;   95
Only your bounteous disposition
Fame hath divulg'd, and is to me well known.

SIR BOUNTEOUS.

    Nay, and your lordship know my disposition, you know
me better than they that know my person; your honor is so
much the welcomer for that.   100

FOLLYWIT.

    Thanks, good Sir Bounteous.

SIR BOUNTEOUS.

    Pray pardon me, it has been often my ambition, my lord,
both in respect of your honorable presence, and the prodigal

81. Why . . . my] *Q1*; and . . . your   92–94. In . . . presume] *Dyce*; In
Q2.   . . . houses/ And . . . presume *Q1–2*.
91. is] *Dyce*; in *Q1*.   97. and is] *Q1*; and it is *Q2*.

fame that keeps even stroke with your unbounded worthiness,
To have wish'd your lordship where your lordship is,   105
A noble guest in this unworthy seat.
Your lordship ne'er heard my organs?

FOLLYWIT.

Heard of 'em, Sir Bounteous, but never heard 'em.

SIR BOUNTEOUS.

They're but double gilt, my lord; some hundred and fifty
pound will fit your lordship with such another pair.   110

FOLLYWIT.

Indeed, Sir Bounteous?

SIR BOUNTEOUS.

Oh, my lord, I have a present suit to you.

FOLLYWIT.

To me, Sir Bounteous? And you could ne'er speak at fitter
time, for I'm here present to grant you.

SIR BOUNTEOUS.

Your lordship has been a traveler?   115

FOLLYWIT.

Some five year, sir.

SIR BOUNTEOUS.

I have a grandchild, my lord. I love him, and when I die I'll
do somewhat for him. I'll tell your honor the worst of him:
a wild lad he has been.

FOLLYWIT.

So we have been all, sir.   120

SIR BOUNTEOUS.

So we have been all indeed, my lord; I thank your lordship's
assistance. Some comic pranks he has been guilty of, but I'll
pawn my credit for him, an honest, trusty bosom.

FOLLYWIT.

And that's worth all, sir.

SIR BOUNTEOUS.

And that's worth all indeed, my lord, for he's like to have   125
all when I die. *Imberbis juvenis*, his chin has no more prickles

126. *Imberbis juvenis*] *Q1; imberdis
Iuvebis Q2.*

---

126. *Imberbis juvenis*] "Beardless youth."

yet than a midwife's; there's great hope of his wit, his hair's
so long a-coming. Shall I be bold with your honor to
prefer this aforesaid Ganymede to hold a plate under your
lordship's cup?   130

FOLLYWIT

You wrong both his worth and your bounty, and you call
that boldness. Sir, I have heard much good of that young
gentleman.

SIR BOUNTEOUS.

Nay, h'as a good wit i'faith, my lord.

FOLLYWIT.

H'as carried himself always generously.   135

SIR BOUNTEOUS.

Are you advis'd of that, my lord? H'as carried many things
cleanly. I'll show your lordship my will; I keep it above in an
outlandish box. The whoreson boy must have all; I love
him, yet he shall ne'er find it as long as I live.

FOLLYWIT.

Well, sir, for your sake and his own deserving, I'll reserve a   140
place for him nearest to my secrets.

SIR BOUNTEOUS.

I understand your good lordship, you'll make him your
secretary. My music, give my lord a taste of his welcome.

A strain play'd by the consort, Sir Bounteous *makes a courtly honor to that
lord and seems to foot the tune.*

SIR BOUNTEOUS.

So, how like you our airs, my lord? Are they choice?

FOLLYWIT.

They're seldom match'd, believe it.   145

SIR BOUNTEOUS.

The consort of mine own household.

FOLLYWIT.

Yea, sir.

---

127. *midwife's*] often used with the sense of "effeminate man."
127–128. *there's . . . a-coming*] "An allusion to the proverb, More hair than
wit" (Bullen).
143.1. *consort*] a company of musicians.

SIR BOUNTEOUS.

>The musicians are in ordinary, yet no ordinary musicians.
>Your lordship shall hear my organs now.

FOLLYWIT.

>Oh, I beseech you, Sir Bounteous. 150

SIR BOUNTEOUS.

>My organist!

The organs play, and cover'd dishes march over the stage.

>Come, my lord, how does your honor relish my organ?

FOLLYWIT.

>A very proud air, i' faith, sir.

SIR BOUNTEOUS.

>Oh, how can 't choose? A Walloon plays upon 'em, and a
>Welshman blows wind in their breech. *Exeunt.* 155

A song to the organs.

[II.ii]

Enter Sir Bounteous *with* Follywit *and his consorts* [Mawworm, Hoboy,
others] *toward his lodging.*

SIR BOUNTEOUS.

>You must pardon us, my lord, hasty cates. Your honor has
>had ev'n a hunting meal on't, and now I am like to bring
>your lordship to as mean a lodging: a hard down bed, i'
>faith, my lord, poor cambric sheets, and a cloth o' tissue
>canopy. The curtains indeed were wrought in Venice, with 5
>the story of the prodigal child in silk and gold; only the
>swine are left out, my lord, for spoiling the curtains.

FOLLYWIT.

>'Twas well prevented, sir.

SIR BOUNTEOUS.

>Silken rest, harmonious slumbers, and venereal dreams to
>your lordship. 10

---

148. *in ordinary*] belonging to the regular household staff.
154. *Walloon . . . 'em*] not clear, but perhaps "vehemently," referring to
the Walloons' reputation as fighters.
155. *Welshman*] The Welsh were noted for their bragging.
[II.ii]
0.1. *consorts*] companions.

FOLLYWIT.

    The like to kind, Sir Bounteous.

SIR BOUNTEOUS.

    Fie, not to me, my lord. I'm old, past dreaming of such
    vanities.

FOLLYWIT.

    Old men should dream best.

SIR BOUNTEOUS.

    They're dreams indeed, my lord, y'ave gi'n't us. Tomorrow   15
    your lordship shall see my cocks, my fish ponds, my park,
    my champaign grounds; I keep champers in my house can
    show your lordship some pleasure.

FOLLYWIT.

    Sir Bounteous, you ev'n whelm me with delights.

SIR BOUNTEOUS.

    Once again a musical night to your honor; I'll trouble your   20
    lordship no more.   *Exit.*

FOLLYWIT.

    Good rest, Sir Bounteous. —So, come, the vizards; where be
    the masking suits?

MAWWORM.

    In your lordship's portmantua.

FOLLYWIT.

    Peace, lieutenant.   25

MAWWORM.

    I had rather have war, captain.

FOLLYWIT.

    Puh, the plot's ripe. Come, to our business, lad;
    Though guilt condemns, 'tis gilt must make us glad.

MAWWORM.

    Nay, and you be at your distinctions, captain, I'll follow
    behind no longer.   30

27. our] *Q 1*; the *Q 2*.

---

17. *champaign grounds*] open fields.
17. *champers*] eaters (?). The word may be a mistake for "chambers." *champaigne*
22. *vizards*] face masks.
24. *portmantua*] portmanteau.
28. *gilt*] gelt, money.

FOLLYWIT.

Get you before then, and whelm your nose with your
   vizard; go.   [*Exit* Mawworm.]
Now, grandsire, you that hold me at hard meat
And keep me out at the dag's end, I'll fit you.
Under his lordship's leave, all must be mine,
He and his will confesses. What I take, then,   35
Is but a borrowing of so much beforehand.
I'll pay him again when he dies in so many blacks;
I'll have the church hung round with a noble a yard,
Or requite him in scutcheons. Let him trap me
In gold, and I'll lap him in lead: *quid pro quo*. I   40
Must look none of his angels in the face, forsooth,
Until his face be not worth looking on. Tut, lads,
Let sires and grandsires keep us low, we must
Live when they're flesh as well as when they're dust.   *Exeunt.*

[II.iii]   *Enter* Courtesan *with her man.*

COURTESAN.

Go, sirrah, run presently to Master Penitent Brothel; you
know his lodging, knock him up. I know he cannot sleep for
sighing.
Tell him I've happily bethought a mean
To make his purpose prosper in each limb,   5
Which only rests to be approv'd by him.
Make haste, I know he thirsts for't.   *Exeunt.*

[II.iv]

A CRY WITHIN.

Oh!

[II.iv]   1. Oh] *Q1*; Oh, oh, oh *Q2*.
1. S.P. A CRY] *this edn.; not in Q1.*

---

33. *dag's end*] at a distance. A dag was a heavy pistol.
37. *blacks*] funeral drapery.
39. *scutcheons*] hatchments, "square or lozenge-shaped tablet[s] exhibiting
the armorial bearings of a deceased person, which [are] affixed to the front
of his dwelling place" (*OED*).
39. *trap*] outfit, clothe.
40. *lap . . . lead*] to wrap a body in lead for burial.
40. *quid . . . quo*] "tit for tat."

Enter, in a masking suit with a vizard in his hand, Follywit.

FOLLYWIT.

Hark, they're at their business.

WITHIN.

Thieves, thieves!

FOLLYWIT.

Gag that gaping rascal! Though he be my grandsire's chief
gentleman i'th' chain of gold, I'll have no pity of him. How   5
now, lads?

    Enter the rest [Mawworm, Hoboy, *others*] *vizarded.*

MAWWORM.

All's sure and safe. On with your vizard, sir; the servants
are all bound.

FOLLYWIT.

There's one care past, then. Come, follow me, lads, I'll lead
you now to th' point and top of all your fortunes. Yon   10
lodging is my grandsire's.

MAWWORM.

So, so, lead on, on.

HOBOY.

Here's a captain worth the following, and a wit worth a
man's love and admiring.   *Exeunt.*

[*Re-*]*enter* [Follywit, Mawworm, Hoboy, *others*] *with* Sir Bounteous *in
his nightgown.*

SIR BOUNTEOUS.

Oh, gentlemen, and you be kind gentlemen, what country-   15
men are you?

FOLLYWIT.

Lincolnshire men, sir.

SIR BOUNTEOUS.

I am glad of that, i' faith.

FOLLYWIT.

And why should you be glad of that?

SIR BOUNTEOUS.

Oh, the honestest thieves of all come out of Lincolnshire, 20
the kindest natur'd gentlemen; they'll rob a man with

3. S.P. WITHIN] *Dyce; First Q1–2.*   12. on, on] *Q1;* on, on, on *Q2.*

conscience, they have a feeling of what they go about, and
will steal with tears in their eyes: ah, pitiful gentlemen.

FOLLYWIT.

Push! Money, money, we come for money.

SIR BOUNTEOUS.

Is that all you come for? Ah, what a beast was I to put out   25
my money t'other day. Alas, good gentlemen, what shift
shall I make for you? Pray come again another time.

FOLLYWIT.

Tut, tut, sir, money.

SIR BOUNTEOUS.

Oh, not so loud, sir, you're too shrill a gentleman. I have
a lord lies in my house; I would not for the world his   30
honor should be disquieted.

FOLLYWIT.

Who, my Lord Owemuch? We have took order with him
beforehand; he lies bound in his bed, and all his followers.

SIR BOUNTEOUS.

Who, my lord? Bound my lord? Alas, what did you mean to
bind my lord? He could keep his bed well enough without   35
binding. Y'ave undone me in't already, you need rob me no
farther.

FOLLYWIT.

Which is the key, come?

SIR BOUNTEOUS.

Ah, I perceive now y'are no true Lincolnshire spirits; you
come rather out of Bedfordshire: we cannot lie quiet in our   40
beds for you. So, take enough, my masters; spur a free
horse, my name's Sir Bounteous. A merry world, i' faith;
what knight but I keep open house at midnight? Well, there
should be a conscience if one could hit upon't.

FOLLYWIT.

Away now; seize upon him, bind him.   45

SIR BOUNTEOUS.

Is this your court of equity? Why should I be bound for

29. so] *Q1*; too *Q2*.

---

25. *put out*] invest.
40. *Bedfordshire*] The rest of the line makes the pun clear.

mine own money? But come, come, bind me, I have need
on't; I have been too liberal tonight. Keep in my hands;
nay, as hard as you list. I am too good to bear my lord
company. You have watch'd your time, my masters; I was   50
knighted at Westminster, but many of these nights will make
me a knight of Windsor. Y'ave deserv'd so well, my masters,
I bid you all to dinner tomorrow; I would I might have
your companies, i' faith; I desire no more.

FOLLYWIT.
   Oh ho, sir!   [*Finds more treasure.*] 55

SIR BOUNTEOUS.
   Pray meddle not with my organs, to put 'em out of tune.

FOLLYWIT.
   Oh no, here's better music.

SIR BOUNTEOUS.
   Ah, pox feast you!

FOLLYWIT.
   Dispatch with him, away. [*Exeunt* Hoboy *and others carrying*
Sir Bounteous.] So, thank you, good grandsire; this was   60
bounteously done of him, i' faith. It came somewhat hard
from him at first, for indeed nothing comes stiff from an old
man but money; and he may well stand upon that when he
has nothing else to stand upon. Where's our portmantua?

MAWWORM.
   Here, bully captain.   65

FOLLYWIT.
   In with the purchase, 'twill lie safe enough there under's
nose, I warrant you. What, is all sure?

     Enter Ancient [Hoboy *and others*].

HOBOY.
   All's sure, captain.

59–60. S.D.] *Exit (after l. 58) Q 1.*   62. comes] *Q 1*; came *Q 2.*

---

  49. *I . . . good*] How good of me.
  52. *knight of Windsor*] gentlemen pensioners, who because of age and
poverty "'are fitter for saying their prayers, than for the service of war'"
(R. B. McKerrow, *Works of Thomas Nashe* [Oxford, 1958], IV, 348).
  66. *purchase*] booty.

FOLLYWIT.

You know what follows now: one villain binds his fellows.
Go, we must be all bound for our own securities, rascals,   70
there's no dallying upo'th' point. You conceit me: there is a
lord to be found bound in the morning, and all his followers;
can you pick out that lord now?

MAWWORM.

Oh admirable spirit!

FOLLYWIT.

You ne'er plot for your safeties, so your wants be satisfied.   75

HOBOY.

But if we bind one another, how shall the last man be
bound?

FOLLYWIT.

Pox on't, I'll have the footman 'scape.

FOOTMAN.

That's I; I thank you, sir.

FOLLYWIT.

The footman, of all other, will be suppos'd to 'scape, for he   80
comes in no bed all night, but lies in's clothes to be first ready
i'th' morning. The horse and he lies in litter together; that's
the right fashion of your bonny footman. And his freedom
will make the better for our purpose, for we must have one
i'th' morning to unbind the knight, that we may have our   85
sport within ourselves. We now arrive at the most ticklish
point, to rob and take our ease, to be thieves and lie by't.
Look to't, lads, it concerns every man's gullet; I'll not have
the jest spoil'd, that's certain, though it hazard a windpipe.
I'll either go like a lord as I came, or be hang'd like a thief   90
as I am; and that's my resolution.

MAWWORM.

Troth, a match, captain, of all hands.   *Exeunt.*

[II.v]   *Enter* Courtesan *with* Master Penitent Brothel.

COURTESAN.

Oh, Master Penitent Brothel!

82. in litter] *Q1*; in's litter *Q2*.   89. the jest] *Q1*; a jest *Q2*.

71. *conceit*] understand.

PENITENT.

    What is't, sweet Lady Gullman, that so seizes on thee with
    rapture and admiration?

COURTESAN.

    A thought, a trick, to make you, sir, especially happy, and
    yet I myself a saver by it.   5

PENITENT.

    I would embrace that, lady, with such courage I would not
    leave you on the losing hand.

COURTESAN.

    I will give trust to you, sir, the cause then why I rais'd you
    from your bed so soon, wherein I know sighs would not let
    you sleep; thus understand it.   10
    You love that woman, Master Harebrain's wife,
    Which no invented means can crown with freedom
    For your desires and her own wish but this,
    Which in my slumbers did present itself.

PENITENT.

    I'm covetous, lady.   15

COURTESAN.

    You know her husband, ling'ring in suspect,
    Locks her from all society but mine.

PENITENT.

    Most true.

COURTESAN.

    I only am admitted, yet hitherto that has done you no real
    happiness; by my admittance I cannot perform that deed   20
    that should please you, you know. Wherefore thus I've
    convey'd it, I'll counterfeit a fit of violent sickness.

PENITENT.

    Good.

COURTESAN.

    Nay, 'tis not so good, by my faith, but to do you good.

PENITENT.

    And in that sense I call'd it. But take me with you, lady;   25

---

13. For your . . . her] *Q1*; For   hitherto/ That . . . admittance/ I . . .
her . . . your *Q2*.   you/ You . . . it/ Ile . . . sicknes
19–22. I . . . sickness] *Dyce*; I . . .   *Q1–2*.

25. *But . . . you*] let me understand you.

would it be probable enough to have a sickness so suddenly violent?

COURTESAN.

Puh, all the world knows women are soon down; we can be sick when we have a mind to't, catch an ague with the wind of our fans, surfeit upon the rump of a lark, and bestow ten 30 pound in physic upon't; we're likest ourselves when we're down. 'Tis the easiest art and cunning for our sect to counterfeit sick, that are always full of fits when we are well; for since we were made for a weak, imperfect creature, we can fit that best that we are made for. I thus translated, and 35 yourself slipp'd into the form of a physician—

PENITENT.

I a physician, lady? Talk not on't, I beseech you; I shall shame the whole college.

COURTESAN.

Tut, man, any quacksalving terms will serve for this purpose; for I am pitifully haunted with a brace of elder brothers, new 40 perfum'd in the first of their fortunes, and I shall see how forward their purses will be to the pleasing of my palate, and restoring of my health. Lay on load enough upon 'em, and spare 'em not, for they're good plump fleshly asses, and may well enough bear it. Let gold, amber, and dissolved 45 pearl be common ingredients, and that you cannot compose a cullis without 'em. Put but this cunningly in practice, it shall be both a sufficient recompense for all my pains in your love, and the ready means to make Mistress Harebrain way, by the visiting of me, to your mutual desired company. 50

PENITENT.

I applaud thee, kiss thee, and will constantly embrace it.

Exeunt.

---

35. best that] *Q1*; best *Q2*.   see *Q2*.
41. shall see] *Q1*; shall presently   49. means] *Q1*; way *Q2*.

32. *sect*] sex.
35. *translated*] transformed.
38. *college*] College of Physicians, examining and qualifying body of the medical profession.
47. *cullis*] strong, nourishing broth.

[II.vi]   *Voices within.*

SIR BOUNTEOUS,
    Ho, Gunwater!
FOLLYWIT.
    Singlestone!
(WITHIN.)
    Jenkin, wa, ha, ho!
(WITHIN.)
    Ewen!
(WITHIN.)
    Simcod!   5
FOLLYWIT.
    Footman! Whew!

Enter Sir Bounteous *with a cord, half unbound,* Footman *with him.*

FOOTMAN.
    Oh, good your worship, let me help your good old worship.
SIR BOUNTEOUS.
    Ah, poor honest footman, how didst thou 'scape this
    massacre?
FOOTMAN.
    E'en by miracle, and lying in my clothes, sir.   10
SIR BOUNTEOUS.
    I think so; I would I had lain in my clothes too, footman,
    so I had 'scap'd 'em; I could have but risse like a beggar
    then, and so I do now, till more money come in. But
    nothing afflicts me so much, my poor geometrical footman,
    as that the barbarous villains should lay violence upon my   15
    lord. Ah, the binding of my lord cuts my heart in two pieces.
    So, so, 'tis well, I thank thee; run to thy fellows, undo 'em,
    undo 'em, undo 'em.
FOOTMAN.
    Alas, if my lord should miscarry, they're unbound already,
    sir; they have no occupation but sleep, feed, and fart.   20
                                                           Exit.

0.1. *Voices within*] *Q1; Voyces singing*   6.1.] *after l. 7 in Q1.*
within Q2.   13. more] *Q1; my Q2.*

---

12. *risse*] risen.
14. *geometrical*] "ground measuring."

SIR BOUNTEOUS.

If I be not asham'd to look my lord i'th' face, I'm a
Saracen. My lord—

FOLLYWIT [*within curtains*].

Who's that?

SIR BOUNTEOUS.

One may see he has been scar'd, a pox on 'em for their
labors.   25

FOLLYWIT.

Singlestone!

SIR BOUNTEOUS.

Singlestone? I'll ne'er answer to that, i' faith.

FOLLYWIT.

Suchman!

SIR BOUNTEOUS.

Suchman? Nor that neither, i' faith; I am not brought so
low, though I be old.   30

FOLLYWIT.

Who's that i'th' chamber?

SIR BOUNTEOUS [*opens curtains*].

Good morrow, my lord, 'tis I.

FOLLYWIT.

Sir Bounteous, good morrow; I would give you my hand,
sir, but I cannot come at it. Is this the courtesy o'th'
country, Sir Bounteous?   35

SIR BOUNTEOUS.

Your lordship grieves me more than all my loss;
'Tis the unnatural'st sight that can be found
To see a noble gentleman hard bound.

FOLLYWIT.

Trust me, I thought you had been better belov'd, Sir
Bounteous; but I see you have enemies, sir, and your friends   40
fare the worse for 'em. I like your talk better than your
lodging; I ne'er lay harder in a bed of down; I have had a

---

23. S.D. *within curtains*] Follywit's bed is probably within the so-called
inner stage, where he is discovered at line 32. The same bed is used by the
courtesan in III.ii, where the stage direction again suggests a discovery.

26. *Singlestone*] Eberle notes Camden's *Remains*, ed. T. Moule (London,
1870), p. 31, where *unstana* ("without stone") means "eunuch."

mad night's rest on't. Can you not guess what they should
be, Sir Bounteous?

SIR BOUNTEOUS.

Faith, Lincolnshire men, my lord.   45

FOLLYWIT.

How? Fie, fie, believe it not, sir; these he not far off, I
warrant you.

SIR BOUNTEOUS.

Think you so, my lord?

FOLLYWIT.

I'll be burnt and they do; some that use to your house, sir,
and are familiar with all the conveyances.   ·   50

SIR BOUNTEOUS.

This is the commodity of keeping open house, my lord, that
makes so many shut their doors about dinner time.

FOLLYWIT.

They were resolute villains. I made myself known to 'em,
told 'em what I was, gave 'em my honorable word not to
disclose 'em—   55

SIR BOUNTEOUS.

Oh saucy, unmannerly villains!

FOLLYWIT.

And think you the slaves would trust me upon my word?

SIR BOUNTEOUS.

They would not?

FOLLYWIT.

Forsooth, no. I must pardon 'em; they told me lords'
promises were mortal, and commonly die within half an   60
hour after they are spoken; they were but gristles, and not
one amongst a hundred come to any full growth or per-
fection, and therefore though I were a lord, I must enter into
bond.

SIR BOUNTEOUS.

Insupportable rascals!   65

---

50. *conveyances*] passageways.
51. *commodity*] profit.
61. *gristles*] "*fig.* with reference to the gristly nature of the bones in
infancy" (*OED*).

FOLLYWIT.

> Troth, I'm of that mind, Sir Bounteous. You far'd the worse
> for my coming hither.

SIR BOUNTEOUS.

> Ah, good my lord, but I'm sure your lordship far'd the
> worse.

FOLLYWIT.

> Pray pity not me, sir.   70

SIR BOUNTEOUS.

> Is not your honor sore about the brawn of the arm? A
> murrain meet 'em, I feel it.

FOLLYWIT.

> About this place, Sir Bounteous?

SIR BOUNTEOUS.

> You feel as it were a twinge, my lord?

FOLLYWIT.

> Ay, e'en a twinge; you say right.   75

SIR BOUNTEOUS.

> A pox discover 'em, that twinge I feel too.

FOLLYWIT.

> But that which disturbs me most, Sir Bounteous, lies here.

SIR BOUNTEOUS.

> True, about the wrist a kind of tumid numbness.

FOLLYWIT.

> You say true, sir.

SIR BOUNTEOUS.

> The reason of that, my lord, is the pulses had no play.   80

FOLLYWIT.

> Mass, so I guess'd it.

SIR BOUNTEOUS.

> A mischief swell 'em, for I feel that too.

> [*Enter* Mawworm.]

MAWWORM.

> 'Slid, here's a house haunted indeed.

SIR BOUNTEOUS [*to* Mawworm].

> A word with you, sir.

---

72. *murrain*] an infectious cattle disease, but used generally as an oath:
"A plague on them."

FOLLYWIT.
How now, Singlestone?   85
MAWWORM.
I'm sorry, my lord, your lordship has lost—
SIR BOUNTEOUS.
Pup, pup, pup, pup, pup!
FOLLYWIT.
What have I lost? Speak!
SIR BOUNTEOUS.
A good night's sleep, say.
FOLLYWIT.
Speak, what have I lost, I say.   90
MAWWORM.
A good night's sleep, my lord, nothing else.
FOLLYWIT.
That's true. My clothes, come!   *Curtains drawn.*
MAWWORM.
My lord's clothes! His honor's rising.
SIR BOUNTEOUS.
Hist, well said. Come hither; what has my lord lost, tell me?
Speak softly.   95
MAWWORM.
His lordship must know that, sir.
SIR BOUNTEOUS.
Hush, prithee tell me.
MAWWORM.
'Twill do you no pleasure to know't, sir.
SIR BOUNTEOUS.
Yet again? I desire it, I say.
MAWWORM.
Since your worship will needs know't, they have stol'n away 100
a jewel in a blue silk riband of a hundred pound price, beside
some hundred pounds in fair spur-royals.
SIR BOUNTEOUS.
That's some two hundred i'th' total.
MAWWORM.
Your worship's much about it, sir.

86. lordship] *Q1*; worship *Q2*.   102. in fair] *Q1*; in a faire *Q2*.

---

102. *spur-royal*] a gold coin worth about fifteen shillings.

SIR BOUNTEOUS.

Come, follow me; I'll make that whole again in so much 105
money. Let not my lord know on't.

MAWWORM.

Oh, pardon me, Sir Bounteous, that were a dishonor to my
lord; should it come to his ear, I should hazard my undoing
by it.

SIR BOUNTEOUS.

How should it come to his ear? If you be my lord's chief man 110
about him, I hope you do not use to speak unless you be paid
for't; and I had rather give you a counselor's double fee to
hold your peace. Come, go to; follow me, I say.

MAWWORM.

There will be scarce time to tell it, sir; my lord will away
instantly. 115

SIR BOUNTEOUS.

His honor shall stay dinner, by his leave; I'll prevail with him
so far. And now I remember a jest: I bade the whoreson
thieves to dinner last night. I would I might have their
companies, a pox poison 'em! *Exit.*

MAWWORM.

Faith, and you are like to have no other guests, Sir Bounte- 120
ous, if you have none but us; I'll give you that gift, i' faith. *Exit.*

Finit Actus Secundus.

[III.i] *Incipit Actus Tertius.*

Enter Master Harebrain *with two elder brothers,* Master Inesse *and*
Master Possibility.

POSSIBILITY.

You see bold guests, Master Harebrain.

HAREBRAIN.

You're kindly welcome to my house, good Master Inesse and
Master Possibility.

120. guests] *Q2;* guesse *Q1.*
121. S.D. *Exit*] *Dyce; Exeunt Q 1–2.*
121.1. *Finit*] *Q1; Finis Q2. Act
division preceded by* A Song, sung by
the musitians, and after the Song, a
Country dance, by the Actors in
their Vizards to a new footing.
Exeunt. *Q2.*

INESSE.

    That's our presumption, sir.

HAREBRAIN.

    Rafe! 5

               [*Enter* Rafe.]

RAFE.

    Here, sir.

HAREBRAIN.

    Call down your mistress to welcome these two gentlemen my
friends.

RAFE.

    I shall, sir. *Exit.*

HAREBRAIN [*aside*].

    I will observe her carriage, and watch 10
The slippery revolutions of her eye;
I'll lie in wait for every glance she gives,
And poise her words i'th' balance of suspect.
If she but swag, she's gone: either on this hand
Overfamiliar, or this too neglectful; 15
It does behove her carry herself even.

POSSIBILITY.

    But Master Harebrain—

HAREBRAIN.

    True, I hear you, sir; was't you said?

POSSIBILITY.

    I have not spoke it yet, sir.

HAREBRAIN.

    Right, so I say. 20

POSSIBILITY.

    Is it not strange that in so short a time my little Lady
Gullman should be so violently handled?

HAREBRAIN.

    Oh, sickness has no mercy, sir.
It neither pities ladies' lip, nor eye;
It crops the rose out of the virgin's cheek, 25
And so deflow'rs her that was ne'er deflowr'd.
Fools, then, are maids to lock from men that treasure

---

14. *swag*] sink down in the balance.
26. *deflow'rs*] Editors note the resemblance to *Romeo and Juliet*, IV.v.37.

Which death will pluck, and never yield 'em pleasure.
Ah, gentlemen, though I shadow it, that sweet virgin's sickness grieves me not lightly; she was my wife's only delight and   30
company. Did you not hear her, gentlemen, i'th' midst of her
extremest fit, still how she call'd upon my wife, remember'd
still my wife, sweet Mistress Harebrain? When she sent for
me, o' one side of her bed stood the physician, the scrivener
on the other; two horrible objects, but mere opposites in the   35
course of their lives, for the scrivener binds folks, and the
physician makes them loose.

POSSIBILITY.

But not loose of their bonds, sir?

HAREBRAIN.

No, by my faith, sir, I say not so. If the physician could
make 'em loose of their bonds, there's many a one would take   40
physic that dares not now for poisoning. But as I was telling
of you, her will was fashioning, wherein I found her best and
richest jewel given as a legacy unto my wife. When I read
that, I could not refrain weeping. Well, of all other, my
wife has most reason to visit her; if she have any good   45
nature in her, she'll show it there.

[*Enter* Rafe.]

Now, sir, where's your mistress?

RAFE.

She desires you and the gentlemen your friends to hold her
excused: sh'as a fit of an ague now upon her, which begins
to shake her.   50

HAREBRAIN.

Where does it shake her most?

RAFE.

All over her body, sir.

HAREBRAIN.

Shake all her body? 'Tis a saucy fit; I'm jealous of that

31–33. Did . . . Harebrain] *Dyce*;   42–43. wherein . . . wife] *Dyce*;
Did . . . midst/ Of . . . wife/ Remem-   Wherein . . . Iewell/ Giuen . . . wife
bred . . . Harebraine *Q 1–2*.   *Q 1–2*.

34. *scrivener*] notary.
35. *mere*] absolute.

ague. Pray walk in, gentlemen, I'll see you instantly.

                     [*Exeunt* Inesse *and* Possibility.]

RAFE.

Now they are absent, sir, 'tis no such thing.   55

HAREBRAIN.

What?

RAFE.

My mistress has her health, sir,
But 'tis her suit she may confine herself
From sight of all men but your own dear self, sir;
For since the sickness of that modest virgin,   60
Her only company, she delights in none.

HAREBRAIN.

No? Visit her again, commend me to her,
Tell her they're gone, and only I myself
Walk here to exchange a word or two with her.

RAFE.

I'll tell her so, sir.   *Exit.*   65

HAREBRAIN.

Fool that I am, and madman, beast! what worse?
Suspicious o'er a creature that deserves
The best opinion and the purest thought;
Watchful o'er her that is her watch herself;
To doubt her ways, that looks too narrowly   70
Into her own defects. I, foolish-fearful,
Have often rudely, out of giddy flames,
Barr'd her those objects which she shuns herself.
Thrice I've had proof of her most constant temper;
Come I at unawares by stealth upon her,   75
I find her circled in with divine writs
Of heavenly meditations; here and there
Chapters with leaves tuck'd up, which when I see,
They either tax pride or adultery.
Ah, let me curse myself, that could be jealous   80
Of her whose mind no sin can make rebellious.
And here the unmatched comes.

79. tax] *Q1*; tax my *Q2*.

[*Enter* Mistress Harebrain.]
                              Now, wife, i' faith they're gone.
Push, see how fearful 'tis; will you not credit me?
They're gone, i' faith; why, think you I'll betray you? Come,
come, thy delight and mine, thy only virtuous friend, thy   85
sweet instructress, is violently taken, grievous sick, and
which is worse, she mends not.

MISTRESS HAREBRAIN.

Her friends are sorry for that, sir.

HAREBRAIN.

She calls still upon thee, poor soul, remembers thee still,
thy name whirls in her breath. "Where's Mistress Hare-   90
brain?" says she.

MISTRESS HAREBRAIN.

Alas, good soul.

HAREBRAIN.

She made me weep thrice; sh'as put thee in a jewel in her
will.

MISTRESS HAREBRAIN.

E'en to th' last gasp a kind soul.   95

HAREBRAIN.

Take my man, go, visit her.

MISTRESS HAREBRAIN.

Pray pardon me, sir; alas, my visitation cannot help her.

HAREBRAIN.

Oh, yet the kindness of a thing, wife. —[*Aside.*] Still she holds
the same rare temper. —Take my man, I say.

MISTRESS HAREBRAIN.

I would not take your man, sir, though I did purpose 100
going.

HAREBRAIN.

No? Thy reason?

MISTRESS HAREBRAIN.

The world's condition is itself so vild, sir,
'Tis apt to judge the worst of those deserve not;
'Tis an ill-thinking age, and does apply   105
All to the form of it own luxury.

---

103. *vild*] vile.
106. *it*] its.
106. *luxury*] lasciviousness.

This censure flies from one, that from another;
That man's her squire, says he; her pimp, the t'other;
She's of the stamp, a third; fourth, I ha' known her.
I've heard this, not without a burning cheek.   110
Then our attires are tax'd, our very gait
Is call'd in question, where a husband's presence
Scatters such thoughts, or makes 'em sink for fear
Into the hearts that breed 'em.
Nay, surely, if I went, sir, I would entreat your company.   115

HAREBRAIN.

Mine? Prithee, wife, I have been there already.

MISTRESS HAREBRAIN.

That's all one; although you bring me but to th' door, sir, I
would entreat no farther.

HAREBRAIN.

Thou'rt such a wife! Why, I will bring thee thither, then,
but not go up, I swear.   120

MISTRESS HAREBRAIN.

I' faith, you shall not; I do not desire it, sir.

HAREBRAIN.

Why then, content.

MISTRESS HAREBRAIN.

Give me your hand you will do so, sir?

HAREBRAIN.

Why, there's my lip I will.

MISTRESS HAREBRAIN.

Why then, I go, sir.   125

HAREBRAIN.

With me or no man, incomparable such a woman.   *Exeunt.*

[III.ii]

Vials, gallipots, plate, and an hourglass by her. The Courtesan *on a bed for
her counterfeit fit. To her,* Master Penitent Brothel, *like a doctor of
physic.*

114. breed] *Q1*; bred *Q2*.

---

109. *of . . . stamp*] "Mistress Harebrain fears that she might be suspected
to be one of those light ladies who 'make the rounds' or 'go current' because
they are recognized as having a price or value" (Eberle).
112. *where*] whereas.
[III.ii]
0.1. *gallipots*] small medicine jars.

PENITENT.

Lady!

COURTESAN.

Ha, what news?

PENITENT.

There's one Sir Bounteous Progress newly alighted from his
foot-cloth, and his mare waits at door, as the fashion is.

COURTESAN.

'Slid, 'tis the knight that privately maintains me; a little   5
short old spiny gentleman in a great doublet?

PENITENT.

The same; I know'm.

COURTESAN.

He's my sole revenue, meat, drink, and raiment. My good
physician, work upon him; I'm weak.

PENITENT.

Enough.   10

[*Enter* Sir Bounteous.]

SIR BOUNTEOUS.

Why, where be these ladies, these plump, soft, delicate
creatures? Ha?

PENITENT.

Who would you visit, sir?

SIR BOUNTEOUS.

Visit, who? What are you with the plague in your mouth?

PENITENT.

A physician, sir.   15

SIR BOUNTEOUS.

Then you are a loose liver, sir; I have put you to your
purgation.

PENITENT [*aside*].

But you need none, you're purg'd in a worse fashion.

---

4. *foot-cloth*] "A large richly ornamented cloth laid over the back of a
horse and hanging to the ground on each side. It was considered as a mark of
dignity and respect" (*OED*).

16. *loose liver*] physicians had a reputation for impiety.

17. *purgation*] proof, trial. "I have made you implicate yourself."

COURTESAN.

    Ah, Sir Bounteous.

SIR BOUNTEOUS.

    How now? What art thou?   20

COURTESAN.

    Sweet Sir Bounteous.

SIR BOUNTEOUS.

    Passion of me, what an alteration's here! Rosamond sick,
old Harry? Here's a sight able to make an old man shrink; I
was lusty when I came in, but I am down now, i' faith.
Mortality! Yea, this puts me in mind of a hole seven foot   25
deep, my grave, my grave, my grave. Hist, master doctor, a
word, sir: hark, 'tis not the plague, is't?

PENITENT.

    The plague, sir? No.

SIR BOUNTEOUS.

    Good.

PENITENT [aside].

    He ne'er asks whether it be the pox or no, and of the twain   30
that had been more likely.

SIR BOUNTEOUS.

    How now, my wench? How dost?

COURTESAN [coughs].

    Huh—weak, knight—huh.

PENITENT [aside].

    She says true: he's a weak knight indeed.

SIR BOUNTEOUS.

    Where does it hold thee most, wench?   35

COURTESAN.

    All parts alike, sir.

PENITENT [aside].

    She says true still, for it holds her in none.

SIR BOUNTEOUS.

    Hark in thine ear, thou'rt breeding of young bones; I am
afraid I have got thee with child, i' faith.

  22–23. *Rosamond . . . Harry*] reference to the romantic story of Rosamund
Clifford, young mistress of old Henry II; she was forced to drink poison by
Henry's queen.

COURTESAN.

    I fear that much, sir.   40

SIR BOUNTEOUS.

    Oh, oh, if it should! A young Progress when all's done.

COURTESAN.

    You have done your good will, sir.

SIR BOUNTEOUS.

    I see by her 'tis nothing but a surfeit of Venus, i' faith, and
though I be old, I have gi'n't her. But since I had the power
to make thee sick, I'll have the purse to make thee whole,   45
that's certain. —Master doctor.

PENITENT.

    Sir?

SIR BOUNTEOUS.

    Let's hear, I pray, what is't you minister to her.

PENITENT.

    Marry, sir, some precious cordial, some costly refocillation,
a composure comfortable and restorative.   50

SIR BOUNTEOUS.

    Ay, ay, that, that, that.

PENITENT.

    No poorer ingredients than the liquor of coral; clear amber,
or *succinum*; unicorn's horn, six grains; *magisterium perlarum*,
one scruple—

51. that, that, that] *Q1*; that, that   52. coral] *Dyce*; Curall *Q1-2*.
Q2.

---

49. *refocillation*] "Restorative, refreshing cordial" (Bullen).
52 ff.] The "quacksalving terms" are taken from contemporary *materia
medica*; the elements share in common their great rarity and cost, and
ability to cure nearly any disease.
52. *liquor . . . coral*] "And the red helpeth ayenste bledynge and ayenste
the fallynge euyll and ayenst the fendes gyle and scorne and ayenst diuers
wonderous doyng, & multiplieth fruite & spedeth begynnyng & endyng
of causes and nedes" (Bartholomeus, Bk. XV [sc. XVI], ch. xxxiii).
52. *amber*] Worn as a necklace, amber cures fever and heals diseases of
the mouth, throat, and jaw; in powder form, it cures ear diseases; it is also
good for eyes and "soveraign for the maladies of the stomacke" (Pliny,
Bk. XXXVII, ch. iii).
53. *magisterium perlarum*] bad Latin for "chief of pearls."
54. *scruple*] one-third of a dram.

SIR BOUNTEOUS.

Ah! 55

PENITENT.

Ossis de corde cervi, half a scruple; *aurum potabile* or his tincture—

SIR BOUNTEOUS.

Very precious, sir.

PENITENT.

All which being finely contunded and mixed in a stone or glass mortar with the spirit of diamber— 60

SIR BOUNTEOUS.

Nay, pray be patient, sir.

PENITENT.

That's impossible; I cannot be patient and a physician too, sir.

SIR BOUNTEOUS.

Oh, cry you mercy, that's true, sir.

PENITENT.

All which aforesaid— 65

SIR BOUNTEOUS.

Ay, there you left, sir.

PENITENT.

When it is almost exsiccate or dry, I add thereto *olei succini, olei masi,* and *cinnamoni.*

SIR BOUNTEOUS.

So, sir, *olei masi;* that same oil of mace is a great comfort to both the Counters. 70

---

55. Ah] *Q1;* Ah, hah *Q2.*

---

56. *Ossis ... cervi*] "Moreover, there are found certaine little bones in the heart and matrice of an hind, and those bee passing good for great bellied women, and such as be in travaile of childe birth" (Pliny, Bk. XXVIII, ch. xix).

56. *aurum potabile*] "drinkable gold," the sovereign remedy.

60. *diamber*] "An old stomachic and cordial containing ambergris, musk, and other aromatics" (*OED*).

67. *olei succini*] "oil of amber."

68. *olei masi*] "oil of mace."

68. *cinnamoni*] "cinnamon."

69. *oil of mace*] "A pun, alluding to the maces which were carried by the serjeants ... when they arrested people" (Dyce).

70. *Counters*] the two debtors' prisons.

PENITENT.

And has been of a long time, sir.

SIR BOUNTEOUS.

Well, be of good cheer, wench; there's gold for thee. —Huh,
let her want for nothing, master doctor; a poor kinswoman of
mine; nature binds me to have a care of her. —[*Aside.*] There
I gull'd you, master doctor. —Gather up a good spirit,   75
wench, the fit will away; 'tis but a surfeit of gristles.—Ha,
ha, I have fitted her; an old knight and a cock o'th' game
still; I have not spurs for nothing, I see.

PENITENT.

No, by my faith, they're hatch'd; they cost you an angel,
sir.   80

SIR BOUNTEOUS.

Look to her, good master doctor, let her want nothing.
I've given her enough already, ha, ha, ha!   *Exit.*

COURTESAN.

So, is he gone?

PENITENT.

He's like himself, gone.

COURTESAN.

Here's somewhat to set up with. How soon he took occasion   85
to slip into his own flattery, soothing his own defects. He
only fears he has done that deed which I ne'er fear'd to come
from him in my life. This purchase came unlook'd for.

PENITENT.

Hist! The pair of sons and heirs.

COURTESAN.

Oh, they're welcome; they bring money.   90

Enter Master Inesse *and* Possibility.

79. cost] *Q1*; lost *Q2*.

---

76. *gristles*] see II.vi.61.n.

77. *fitted*] Looks back to "fit" of line 76: "I'm the one who has produced
this 'illness'."

79. *hatch'd*] inlaid, with a pun pointed out by Eberle: the spur, or spur-
royal, a coin worth fifteen shillings, produces angels, coins worth ten
shillings.

88. *purchase*] profit.

POSSIBILITY.
   Master doctor.

PENITENT.
   I come to you, gentlemen.

POSSIBILITY.
   How does she now?

PENITENT.
   Faith, much after one fashion, sir.

INESSE.
   There's hope of life, sir?   95

PENITENT.
   I see no signs of death of her.

POSSIBILITY.
   That's some comfort. Will she take anything yet?

PENITENT.
   Yes, yes, yes, she'll take still: sh'as a kind of facility in
   taking. How comes your band bloody, sir?

INESSE.
   You may see I met with a scab, sir.   100

PENITENT.
   Diversa genera scabierum, as Pliny reports, there are divers
   kind of scabs.

INESSE.
   Pray let's hear 'em, sir.

PENITENT.
   An itching scab, that is your harlot; a sore scab, your usurer;
   a running, your promoter; a broad scab, your intelligencer;   105
   but a white scab, that's a scald knave and a pander. But to
   speak truth, the only scabs we are nowadays troubled
   withal, are new officers.

---

96. of her] *Q1*; in her *Q2*.   *Q2*.
99. band] *Q1*; hand *Q2*.   108. officers] *Q1*; Officers and
105. running] *Q1*; running scab   Projectors *Q2*.

---

   96. *death of*] death in.
   99. *band*] a wide collar often worn with the ruff.
   101–102. *Diversa . . . scabs*] "Vlcers as they be of many sorts, so are they
cured after divers manners" (Pliny, Bk. XXVI, ch. xiv). In Latin, "Ulcera
multorum sunt generum ac multis modis curantur" (Eberle).
   105. *promoter*] professional informer.
   106. *scald*] "affected with the 'scall'; scabby" (*OED*).

INESSE.

Why, now you come to mine, sir, for I'll be sworn one of
them was very busy about my head this morning; and he   110
should be a scab by that, for they are ambitious and covet
the head.

PENITENT.

Why, you saw I deriv'd him, sir.

INESSE.

You physicians are mad gentlemen.

PENITENT.

We physicians see the most sights of any men living. Your   115
astronomers look upward into th' air, we look downward
into th' body, and indeed we have power upward and
downward.

INESSE.

That you have, i' faith, sir.

POSSIBILITY.

Lady, how cheer you now?   120

COURTESAN.

The same woman still—huh.

POSSIBILITY.

That's not good.   [*Gives money.*]

COURTESAN.

Little alteration. Fie, fie, you have been too lavish, gentlemen.

INESSE.

Puh, talk not of that, lady, thy health's worth a million. 125
Here, master doctor, spare for no cost.

POSSIBILITY.

Look what you find there, sir.

COURTESAN.

What do you mean, gentlemen? Put up, put up; you see I'm
down and cannot strive with you; I would rule you else. You
have me at advantage, but if ever I live, I will requite it   130
deeply.

---

113. *deriv'd*] traced his lineage.
117–118. *power . . . downward*] i.e., from both kinds of purging.

INESSE.

Tut, an't come to that once, we'll requite ourselves well
enough.

POSSIBILITY.

Mistress Harebrain, lady, is setting forth to visit you too.

COURTESAN.

Ha?—huh.   135

PENITENT [*aside*].

There struck the minute that brings forth the birth of all my
joys and wishes. But see the jar now! How shall I rid these
from her?

COURTESAN.

Pray, gentlemen, stay not above an hour from my sight.

INESSE.

'Sfoot, we are not going, lady.   140

PENITENT [*aside*].

Subtly brought about, yet 'twill not do: they'll stick by't.
—A word with you, gentlemen.

BOTH.

What says master doctor?

PENITENT.

She wants but settling of her sense with rest. One hour's
sleep, gentlemen, would set all parts in tune.   145

POSSIBILITY.

He says true, i' faith.

INESSE.

Get her to sleep, master doctor; we'll both sit here and watch
by her.

PENITENT [*aside*].

Hell's angels watch you! No art can prevail with 'em.
What with the thought of joys, and sight of crosses, my   150
wits are at Hercules' Pillars, *non plus ultra*.

COURTESAN.

Master doctor, master doctor!

136. minute] *Q2*; munit *Q1*.   *Q1*.
139. gentlemen] *Dyce*; gentleman   145. would] *Q1*; will *Q2*.

---

151. *Hercules' Pillars*] Gibraltar and Mt. Abyla, the traditional limit to
navigation (*non plus ultra*, "no farther").

PENITENT.

Here, lady.

COURTESAN.

Your physic works; lend me your hand.

POSSIBILITY.

Farewell, sweet lady.   155

INESSE.

Adieu, master doctor.   [*Exeunt* Possibility *and* Inesse.]

COURTESAN.

So.

PENITENT.

Let me admire thee!
The wit of man wanes and decreases soon,
But women's wit is ever at full moon.   160

Enter Mistress Harebrain.

There shot a star from heaven;
I dare not yet behold my happiness,
The splendor is so glorious and so piercing.

COURTESAN

Mistress Harebrain, give my wit thanks hereafter; your
wishes are in sight, your opportunity spacious.   165

MISTRESS HAREBRAIN.

Will you but hear a word from me?

COURTESAN.

Whooh!

MISTRESS HAREBRAIN.

My husband himself brought me to th' door, walks below
for my return. Jealousy is prick-ear'd, and will hear the
wagging of a hair.   170

COURTESAN.

Pish, y'are a faint liver. Trust yourself with your pleasure,
and me with your security; go

PENITENT.

The fullness of my wish!

MISTRESS HAREBRAIN.

Of my desire!

159. wanes] *Q1*; waves *Q2*.

PENITENT.

Beyond this sphere I never will aspire.

Exeunt [Penitent *and* Mistress Harebrain].

Enter Master Harebrain *listening*.

HAREBRAIN.

I'll listen, now the flesh draws nigh her end;   175
At such a time women exchange their secrets
And ransack the close corners of their hearts.
What many years hath whelm'd, this hour imparts.

COURTESAN.

Pray sit down, there's a low stool. Good Mistress Harebrain,
this was kindly done;—huh—give me your hand;—huh— 180
alas, how cold you are. Ev'n so is your husband, that worthy,
wise gentleman; as comfortable a man to woman in my case
as ever trod—huh—shoe-leather. Love him, honor him,
stick by him; he lets you want nothing that's fit for a
woman; and to be sure on't, he will see himself that you 185
want it not.

HAREBRAIN.

And so I do, i' faith, 'tis right my humor.

COURTESAN.

You live a lady's life with him, go where you will, ride
when you will, and do what you will.

HAREBRAIN.

Not so, not so neither; she's better look'd to.   190

COURTESAN.

I know you do, you need not tell me that. 'Twas e'en pity of
your life, i' faith, if ever you should wrong such an innocent
gentleman. Fie, Mistress Harebrain, what do you mean?
Come you to discomfort me? Nothing but weeping with you?

HAREBRAIN.

She's weeping, 't'as made her weep. My wife shows her good 195
nature already.

COURTESAN.

Still, still weeping? —[*Sobs.*] Huff, huff, huff. —Why, how
now, woman? Hey, hy, hy, for shame, leave. —Suh, suh.

—She cannot answer me for snobbing.

HAREBRAIN.

All this does her good. Beshrew my heart and I pity her; let 200
her shed tears till morning, I'll stay for her. She shall have
enough on't by my good will; I'll not be her hindrance.

COURTESAN.

Oh no, lay your hand here, Mistress Harebrain. Ay, there;
oh, there, there lies my pain, good gentlewoman. Sore? Oh,
ay, I can scarce endure your hand upon't. 205

HAREBRAIN.

Poor soul, how she's tormented.

COURTESAN.

Yes, yes, I eat a cullis an hour since.

HAREBRAIN.

There's some comfort in that yet; she may 'scape it.

COURTESAN.

Oh, it lies about my heart much.

HAREBRAIN.

I'm sorry for that, i' faith; she'll hardly 'scape it. 210

COURTESAN.

Bound? No, no, I'd a very comfortable stool this morning.

HAREBRAIN.

I'm glad of that, i' faith, that's a good sign; I smell she'll
'scape it now.

COURTESAN.

Will you be going then?

HAREBRAIN.

Fall back, she's coming. 215

COURTESAN.

Thanks, good Mistress Harebrain; welcome, sweet Mistress
Harebrain; pray commend me to the good gentleman your
husband—

HAREBRAIN.

I could do that myself now.

203. hand here] *Q1*; hand on heere   210. sorry for] *Q1*; glad of *Q2*.
Q2.

---

199. *snobbing*] sobbing.

COURTESAN.

And to my Uncle Winchcomb, and to my Aunt Lipsalve, 220
and to my Cousin Falsetop, and to my Cousin Lickit, and to
my Cousin Horseman, and to all my good cousins in
Clerkenwell and St. Johns's.

Enter Wife *with* Master Penitent.

MISTRESS HAREBRAIN.

At three days' end my husband takes a journey.

PENITENT.

Oh, thence I derive a second meeting.   225

MISTRESS HAREBRAIN.

May it prosper still;
Till then I rest a captive to his will.
Once again, health, rest, and strength to thee, sweet lady.
Farewell, you witty squall. Good master doctor, have a care
to her body; if you stand her friend, I know you can do her 230
good.

COURTESAN.

Take pity of your waiter, go. Farewell, sweet Mistress
Harebrain.   [*Exit.*]

HAREBRAIN.

Welcome, sweet wife, alight upon my lip. Never was hour
spent better.   235

MISTRESS HAREBRAIN.

Why, were you within the hearing, sir?

HAREBRAIN.

Ay, that I was, i' faith, to my great comfort; I deceiv'd you
there, wife, ha, ha!
I do entreat thee, nay, conjure thee, wife,
Upon my love or what can more be said,   240
Oft'ner to visit this sick, virtuous maid.

230. you stand] *Q2*; yous stand *Q1.*

220–222. *Uncle . . . cousins*] Compare Dekker and Webster's *Westward Ho!*,
1607, sig. F1v (IV.i.156–158): "O excellent mistris *Bird* [*lime*] thou hast
more trickes in thee then a Puncke hath Vncles, cosins, Brothers, Sons or
Fathers: an infinit Company."
   223. *Clerkenwell . . . St. Johns's*] The Priory of St. Johns was the main
landmark in the district of Clerkenwell, which had a bad reputation as a
haunt of thieves and prostitutes.

MISTRESS HAREBRAIN.

Be not so fierce; your will shall be obey'd.

HAREBRAIN.

Why then, I see thou lov'st me.   *Exeunt* [Harebrains].

PENITENT.

Art of ladies!

When plots are e'en past hope and hang their head,   245
Set with a woman's hand, they thrive and spread.   *Exit.*

[III.iii]

Enter Follywit *with* Lieutenant Mawworm, Ancient Hoboy, *and the rest of his consorts.*

FOLLYWIT.

Was't not well manag'd, you necessary mischiefs? Did the plot want either life or art?

MAWWORM.

'Twas so well, captain, I would you could make such another muss at all adventures.

FOLLYWIT.

Dost call't a muss? I am sure my grandsire ne'er got his   5
money worse in his life than I got it from him. If ever he did
cozen the simple, why I was born to revenge their quarrel;
if ever oppress the widow, I, a fatherless child, have done as
much for him. And so 'tis through the world either in jest or
earnest. Let the usurer look for't; for craft recoils in the end,   10
like an overcharg'd musket, and maims the very hand that
puts fire to't. There needs no more but a usurer's own blow to
strike him from hence to hell; 'twill set him forward with a
vengeance. But here lay the jest, whoresons: my grandsire,
thinking in his conscience that we had not robb'd him   15
enough o'ernight, must needs pity me i'th' morning and
give me the rest.

MAWWORM.

Two hundred pounds in fair rose nobles, I protest.

[III.iii]
0.1. Hoboy] *Q1; Hobby Q2.*

[III.iii]
   4. *muss*] scramble.
  18. *rose noble*] gold coin worth about sixteen shillings.

FOLLYWIT.

Push, I knew he could not sleep quietly till he had paid me
for robbing of him, too; 'tis his humor, and the humor of 20
most of your rich men in the course of their lives; for you
know they always feast those mouths that are least needy,
and give them more that have too much already. And
what call you that but robbing of themselves a courtlier
way? Oh!   25

MAWWORM.

Cuds me, how now, captain?

FOLLYWIT.

A cold fit that comes over my memory and has a shrode pull
at my fortunes.

MAWWORM.

What's that, sir?

FOLLYWIT.

Is it for certain, lieutenant, that my grandsire keeps an 30
uncertain creature, a quean?

MAWWORM.

Ay, that's too true, sir.

FOLLYWIT.

So much the more preposterous for me; I shall hop shorter
by that trick: she carries away the thirds at least. 'Twill prove
entail'd land, I am afraid, when all's done, i' faith. Nay, I 35
have known a vicious, old, thought-acting father,
Damn'd only in his dreams, thirsting for game
(When his best parts hung down their heads for shame)
For his blanch'd harlot dispossess his son
And make the pox his heir; 'twas gravely done.   40
How hadst thou first knowledge on't, lieutenant?

22. those] *Q1*; their *Q2*.   30. Is it] *Q1*; It is *Q2*.
27. shrode] *Q1*; shroud *Q2*.   30. keeps] *Q1*; kept *Q2*.

---

27. *shrode*] shrewd, sharp.
31. *quean*] jade, hussy.
33. *preposterous*] in its etymological sense of "placing last what should
come first."
35. *entail'd*] having limits as to its transference.
36. *thought-acting*] capable of the sepual act only in imagination.
39. *blanch'd*] whitened by cosmetics. The word had a pejorative connota-
tion in the fifteenth–seventeenth centuries.
40. *pox*] syphilis.

MAWWORM.

    Faith, from discourse; yet all the policy
    That I could use, I could not get her name.

FOLLYWIT.

    Dull slave, that ne'er couldst spy it!

MAWWORM.

    But the manner of her coming was describ'd to me.   45

FOLLYWIT.

    How is the manner, prithee?

MAWWORM.

    Marry, sir, she comes most commonly coach'd.

FOLLYWIT.

    Most commonly coach'd indeed; for coaches are as common
    nowadays as some that ride in 'em. She comes most com-
    monly coach'd—   50

MAWWORM.

    True, there I left, sir;—guarded with some leash of pimps.

FOLLYWIT.

    Beside the coachman?

MAWWORM.

    Right, sir. Then alighting, she's privately receiv'd by
    Master Gunwater.

FOLLYWIT.

    That's my grandsire's chief gentleman i'th' chain of gold.   55
    That he should live to be a pander, and yet look upon his
    chain and his velvet jacket!

MAWWORM.

    Then is your grandsire rounded i'th' ear, the key given
    after the Italian fashion, backward, she closely convey'd
    into his closet, there remaining till either opportunity smile   60
    upon his credit, or he send down some hot caudle to take
    order in his performance.

FOLLYWIT.

    Peace, 'tis mine own, i' faith; I ha't!

---

47. *most . . . coach'd*] Eberle quotes Stow, *Annales* (London, 1631), p. 867,
that in 1605 "began the ordinary use of Caroaches."
    58. *rounded*] whispered.
    61. *caudle*] warm, spiced restorative drink.

MAWWORM.

How now, sir?

FOLLYWIT.   Thanks, thanks to any spirit

That mingled it 'mongst my inventions!   65

HOBOY.

Why, Master Follywit!

ALL.

Captain!

FOLLYWIT.

Give me scope and hear me.

I have begot that means which will both furnish me,

And make that quean walk under his conceit.   70

MAWWORM.

That were double happiness, to put thyself into money and
her out of favor.

FOLLYWIT.

And all at one dealing!

HOBOY.

'Sfoot, I long to see that hand play'd.

FOLLYWIT.

And thou shalt see't quickly, i' faith; nay, 'tis in grain, I   75
warrant it hold color. Lieutenant, step behind yon hanging;
if I mistook not at my entrance there hangs the lower part of
a gentlewoman's gown, with a mask and a chin-clout; bring
all this way. Nay, but do't cunningly now; 'tis a friend's
house and I'd use it so—there's a taste for you.   80

[*Exit* Mawworm.]

HOBOY.

But prithee what wilt thou do with a gentlewoman's lower
part?

FOLLYWIT.

Why, use it.

---

70. *walk . . . conceit*] sink in his estimation.

75. *in grain*] i.e., fast-dyed. "*Grain* is the regular word for the red dye
derived from the *coccus* insect (cochineal), which, when dried, looks like a
kind of grain" (G. L. Kittredge, ed., *Twelfth Night*, I.v.256).

77–78. *lower . . . gown*] skirt or kirtle.

78. *chin-clout*] muffler.

80. *there's . . . you*] Perhaps directed to the audience.

HOBOY.

> Y'ave answered me indeed in that; I can demand no
> farther.   85

FOLLYWIT.

> Well said. Lieutenant—

[*Enter* Mawworm.]

MAWWORM.

> What will you do now, sir?

FOLLYWIT.

> Come, come, thou shalt see a woman quickly made up here.

MAWWORM.

> But that's against kind, captain, for they are always long
> a-making ready.   90

FOLLYWIT.

> And is not most they do against kind, I prithee? To lie with
> their horse-keeper, is not that against kind? To wear half-
> moons made of another's hair, is not that against kind? To
> drink down a man, she that should set him up, pray is not that
> monstrously against kind, now? Nay, over with it, lieutenant,   95
> over with it; ever while you live put a woman's clothes over
> her head. Cupid plays best at blindman buff.

MAWWORM.

> You shall have your will, maintenance; I love mad tricks as
> well as you for your heart, sir. But what shift will you make
> for upper bodies, captain?   100

FOLLYWIT.

> I see now thou'rt an ass. Why, I'm ready.

MAWWORM.

> Ready?

92–93. half-moons] *Q1*; Periwigs   98. maintenance] *Q1*; maintayned
Q2.   *Q2*.

---

89. *kind*] nature.

92–93. *half-moons*] wigs, perhaps transformations to make the natural head
of hair fuller.

98. *maintenance*] see I.i.8.

100. *upper bodies*] bodice. "Beginning in the [1580's] the bodies were
made so much like the masculine doublet, that distinguishing them was
difficult" (Linthicum, p. 178).

FOLLYWIT.

Why, the doublet serves as well as the best, and is most in
fashion. We're all male to th' middle, mankind from the
beaver to th' bum. 'Tis an Amazonian time; you shall have 105
women shortly tread their husbands. I should have a couple
of locks behind; prithee, lieutenant, find 'em out for me, and
wind 'em about my hatband. Nay, you shall see, we'll be in
fashion to a hair, and become all with probability; the most
musty-visage critic shall not except against me.   110

MAWWORM.

Nay, I'll give thee thy due behind thy back; thou art as mad
a piece of clay—

FOLLYWIT.

Clay! Dost call thy captain clay? Indeed, clay was made to
stop holes, he says true. Did not I tell you rascals you should
see a woman quickly made up?   115

HOBOY.

I'll swear for't, captain.

FOLLYWIT.

Come, come, my mask and my chin-clout. Come into th'
court.

MAWWORM.

Nay, they were both i'th' court long ago, sir.

FOLLYWIT.

Let me see; where shall I choose two or three for pimps now? 120
But I cannot choose amiss amongst you all, that's the best.
Well, as I am a quean, you were best have a care of me and
guard me sure; I give you warning beforehand, 'tis a
monkey-tail'd age. Life, you shall go nigh to have half a
dozen blithe fellows surprise me cowardly, carry me away 125
with a pair of oars, and put in at Putney.

109. all with] *Q1*; with all *Q2*.

---

105. *beaver ... bum*] hat to waist. A bum was a French farthingale, "a
roll resembling an automobile tire, stiffened by wire, or stuffed with
cotton ... placed around the hips" (Linthicum, p. 181).

110. *except against*] object to.

124. *monkey-tail'd*] lecherous.

126, 128. *Putney, Cue*] Small towns west of London on the Surrey bank,
noted as pleasure haunts. (Cue is Kew.) Middleton makes a typically
indecent use of the initials.

MAWWORM.

> We should laugh at that, i' faith.

FOLLYWIT.

> Or shoot in upo'th' coast of Cue.

MAWWORM.

> Two notable fit landing places for lechers, P. and C.,
> Putney and Cue. 130

FOLLYWIT.

> Well, say you have fair warning on't. The hair about the
> hat is as good as a flag upo'th' pole at a common playhouse
> to waft company, and a chin-clout is of that powerful
> attraction, I can tell you, 'twill draw more linen to't.

MAWWORM.

> Fear not us, captain; there's none here but can fight for a 135
> whore as well as some Inns o' Court man.

FOLLYWIT.

> Why then, set forward, and as you scorn two-shilling brothel,
> Twelve-penny panderism, and such base bribes,
> Guard me from bonny scribs and bony scribes.

MAWWORM.

> Hang 'em, pensions and allowances, fourpence halfpenny 140
> a meal, hang 'em! *Exeunt.*

Finit Actus Tertius.

---

137. shilling] *Q1*; shillings *Q2*.
138–139.] *Dyce; prose in Q1–2.*

139. scribes] *Q1*; Scribes, and bony rags *Q2*.
141.1. *Finit*] *Q1*; *Finis Q2*.

132–133. *flag . . . company*] see I.i.35.n.
134. *'twill . . . to't*] Not clear. In Middleton's *Father Hubburd's Tales* there are references to courtesans dressed as laundresses and to bawds dressed as starchwomen.
136. *Inns o' Court man*] law student. Justice Shallow remembers the rowdy times of his fellow law students, when he was "lusty Shallow" (*2 Henry IV*, III ii.14–38).
137. *two-shilling brothel*] "Halfe a Crowne [two shillings and sixpence] or a little more (or some-times lesse) is the sette pryce of a strumpets soule" (McKerrow, *Works of Thomas Nashe*, II, 149).
139. *scribs*] Not clear; *OED* suggests "miser." Perhaps "scholarly drudge" (see Burton's *Anatomy of Melancholy*, I.ii.3.15).

[IV.i]   *Incipit Actus Quartus.*

Enter in his chamber out of his study, Master Penitent Brothel, *a book in his hand, reading.*

PENITENT.

    Ha! Read that place again. "Adultery
    Draws the divorce 'twixt heaven and the soul."
    Accursed man, that stand'st divorc'd from heaven,
    Thou wretched unthrift, that hast play'd away
    Thy eternal portion at a minute's game   5
    To please the flesh, hast blotted out thy name,
    Where were thy nobler meditations busied
    That they durst trust this body with itself,
    This natural drunkard that undoes us all
    And makes our shame apparent in our fall?   10
    Then let my blood pay for't, and vex and boil.
    My soul, I know, would never grieve to th' death
    The eternal spirit that feeds her with his breath.
    Nay, I that knew the price of life and sin,
    What crown is kept for continence, what for lust,   15
    The end of man, and glory of that end
    As endless as the giver,
    To dote on weakness, slime, corruption, woman!
    What is she, took asunder from her clothes?
    Being ready, she consists of hundred pieces   20
    Much like your German clock, and near allied:
    Both are so nice they cannot go for pride,
    Beside a greater fault, but too well known,
    They'll strike to ten when they should stop at one.
    Within these three days the next meeting's fix'd;   25
    If I meet then, hell and my soul be mix'd.
    My lodging I know constantly, she not knows.
    Sin's hate is the best gift that sin bestows;

0.2. Brothel] *Once-Ill Q1–2 (see In-*   21. clock] *Q2;* cloak *Q1 (corr.);*
tro., p. xviii).   clack *Q1 (uncorr.).*

1–29.] The speech of remorse is common in Middleton's plays; see *A Chaste Maid in Cheapside,* V.i.67 ff., *The Spanish Gypsy,* III.i.1 ff.

21. *German clock*] "An allusion to the cumbersome and complicated machinery of our first clocks, which came from Germany" (Dyce).

I'll ne'er embrace her more; never, bear witness, never.

Enter the devil [as Succubus] *in her shape, claps him on the shoulder*

SUCCUBUS.

What, at a stand? The fitter for my company.   30

PENITENT.

Celestial soldiers guard me!

SUCCUBUS.

                              How now, man?
'Las, did the quickness of my presence fright thee?

PENITENT.

Shield me, you ministers of faith and grace!

SUCCUBUS.

Leave, leave; are you not asham'd to use
Such words to a woman?   35

PENITENT.

Th'art a devil.

SUCCUBUS.

                              A devil?
Feel, feel, man; has a devil flesh and bone?

PENITENT.

I do conjure thee by that dreadful power—

SUCCUBUS.

The man has a delight to make me tremble.
Are these the fruits of thy adventurous love?   40
Was I entic'd for this? to be soon rejected?
Come, what has chang'd thee so, delight?

PENITENT.

                                          Away!

SUCCUBUS.

Remember—

PENITENT.

                    Leave my sight!

---

29. bear] *Dyce*; better *Q1–2*.   36–37. A . . . bone] *one line in Q1–2*.
34–35.] *prose in Q1–2*.

29.1. *Succubus*] "A demon in female form supposed to have carnal intercourse with men in their sleep" (*OED*).

30. *at a stand*] "Idleness is the devil's workshop."

37. *has . . . bone*] A question that bothered academics was whether evil spirits were palpable or not. Reginald Scot summarizes many arguments in his *Discovery of Witchcraft* (1584), ch. 4.

SUCCUBUS.

    Have I this meeting wrought with cunning
    Which, when I come, I find thee shunning?   45
    Rouse thy amorous thoughts and twine me;
    All my interest I resign thee.
    Shall we let slip this mutual hour
    Comes so seldom in her power?
    Where's thy lip, thy clip, thy fadom?   50
    Had women such loves, would't not mad 'em?
    Art a man? or dost abuse one?
    A love? and knowst not how to use one?
    Come, I'll teach thee.

PENITENT.
                    Do not follow!

SUCCUBUS.

    Once so firm, and now so hollow?   55
    When was place and season sweeter?
    Thy bliss in sight, and dar'st not meet her?
    Where's thy courage, youth, and vigor?
    Love's best pleas'd when't's seiz'd with rigor;
    Seize me then with veins most cheerful,   60
    Women love no flesh that's fearful.
    'Tis but a fit, come, drink't away,
    And dance and sing, and kiss and play.
    Fa le la, le la, fa le la, le la la,   *[Dances about him.]*
    Fa le la, fa la le, la le la!   65

PENITENT.
    Torment me not!

SUCCUBUS.
    Fa le la, fa le la, fa la la loh!

---

51. would't] *Q1* (*corr.*); wouldst *Q1*   59. seiz'd] *Dyce*; seard *Q1–2*.
(*uncorr.*).   60. Seize] *Dyce*; Ceare *Q1*; Seare
58. Where's] *Q1* (*corr.*); Whers *Q1*   *Q2*.
(*uncorr.*).

---

    50. *fadom*] fathom, embrace. "Clip" and "fadom" are synonyms.
    59. *seiz'd*] In Middleton's secretary hand *z* looks very much like *r*; a
similar misreading occurs in *The Family of Love*, IV.iv.6, "Nay, ready to
have seiz'd th'expected prize," where the quarto reads "feard." (See
textual notes for ll. 59, 60.)

PENITENT.

Fury!

SUCCUBUS.

Fa le la, fa le la, fa la la loh!

PENITENT.

Devil! I do conjure thee once again,   70
By that soul-quaking thunder, to depart
And leave this chamber freed from thy damn'd art.

Succubus stamps and exit.

PENITENT.

It has prevail'd. Oh, my sin-shaking sinews!
What should I think? Jasper, why, Jasper!

[Enter Jasper.]

JASPER.

Sir! How now? What has disturb'd you, sir?   75

PENITENT.

A fit, a qualm. Is Mistress Harebrain gone?

JASPER.

Who, sir? Mistress Harebrain?

PENITENT.

Is she gone, I say?

JASPER.

Gone? Why, she was never here yet.

PENITENT.

No?   80

JASPER.

Why no, sir.

PENITENT.

Art sure on't?

JASPER.

Sure on't? If I be sure I breathe and am myself.

PENITENT.

I like it not. Where kept'st thou?

JASPER.

I'th' next room, sir.   85

77. Harebrain] *Hargraue Q 1–2*
Intro., p. xviii).

PENITENT.

Why, she struck by thee, man.

JASPER.

You'd make one mad, sir; that a gentlewoman should steal
by me and I not hear her! 'Sfoot, one may hear the ruffling
of their bums almost an hour before we see 'em.

PENITENT.

I will be satisfied, although to hazard.   90
What though her husband meet me? I am honest.
When men's intents are wicked, their guilt haunts 'em,
But when they're just they're arm'd, and nothing daunts 'em.

JASPER [aside].

What strange humor call you this? He dreams of women
and both his eyes broad open!   Exeunt.   95

[IV.ii]   Enter at one door Sir Bounteous, at another Gunwater.

SIR BOUNTEOUS.

Why, how now, Master Gunwater? What's the news with
your haste?

GUNWATER.

I have a thing to tell your worship.

SIR BOUNTEOUS.

Why, prithee tell me; speak, man.

GUNWATER.

Your worship shall pardon me, I have better bringing up   5
than so.

SIR BOUNTEOUS.

How, sir?

GUNWATER.

'Tis a thing made fit for your ear, sir.

SIR BOUNTEOUS.

Oh, oh, oh, cry you mercy; now I begin to taste you. Is she
come?   10

GUNWATER.

She's come, sir.

[IV.ii]   from this point [sig. F3] to end of both
0.1. Gunwater] Gumwater Q1–2 (so   quarto texts; see Intro., p. xix).

---

89. bums] see III.iii.105.n.
[IV.ii]
  9. taste] "understand," but also "approve of, enjoy."

SIR BOUNTEOUS.

Recover'd, well and sound again?

GUNWATER.

That's to be fear'd, sir.

SIR BOUNTEOUS.

Why, sir?

GUNWATER.

She wears a linen cloth about her jaw.   15

SIR BOUNTEOUS.

Ha, ha, haw! Why, that's the fashion, you whoreson
Gunwater.

GUNWATER.

The fashion, sir?
Live I so long time to see that a fashion
Which rather was an emblem of dispraise?   20
It was suspected much in Monsieur's days.

SIR BOUNTEOUS.

Ay, ay, in those days; that was a queasy time. Our age is
better harden'd now and put oft'ner in the fire: we are tried
what we are. Tut, the pox is as natural now as an ague in the
springtime; we seldom take physic without it. Here, take   25
this key, you know what duties belong to't. Go, give order
for a cullis; let there be a good fire made i'th' matted chamber, do you hear, sir?

GUNWATER.

I know my office, sir.   *Exit.*

SIR BOUNTEOUS.

An old man's venery is very chargeable, my masters; there's 30
much cookery belongs to't.   *Exit.*

[IV.iii]

Enter Gunwater *with* Follywit *in courtesan's disguise, and mask'd.*

GUNWATER.

Come, lady, you know where you are now?

18–19. The . . . fashion] *Dyce; one*   25. take physic] *Q1;* Physicke *Q2.*
line in Q1–2.   26. know] *Q2;* knew *Q1.*

---

15. *linen . . . jaw*] Gunwater thinks she is disguising the effects of syphilis.
21. *Monsieur's days*] The Duke of Anjou, brother of Charles IX of France,
visited England in 1581, hoping to marry Elizabeth.
30. *venery*] "lechery," but also "hunting." The speech is addressed to the
audience.

FOLLYWIT.
Yes, good Master Gunwater.

GUNWATER.
This is the old closet, you know.

FOLLYWIT.
I remember it well, sir.

GUNWATER.
There stands a casket. I would my yearly revenue were but   5
worth the wealth that's lock'd in't, lady; yet I have fifty
pound a year, wench.

FOLLYWIT.
Beside your apparel, sir?

GUNWATER.
Yes, faith, have I.

FOLLYWIT.
But then you reckon your chain, sir.   10

GUNWATER.
No, by my troth, do I not neither. Faith, and you consider
me rightly, sweet lady, you might admit a choice gentleman
into your service.

FOLLYWIT.
Oh, pray away, sir.

GUNWATER.
Pusha, come, come, you do but hinder your fortunes, i' faith.   15
I have the command of all the house; I can tell you, nothing
comes into th' kitchen but comes through my hands.

FOLLYWIT.
Pray do not handle me, sir.

GUNWATER.
Faith, y'are too nice, lady. And as for my secrecy, you know
I have vow'd it often to you.   20

FOLLYWIT.
Vow'd it? No, no, you men are fickle.

GUNWATER.
Fickle? 'Sfoot, bind me, lady.

16. have the] *Q1*; have *Q2*.

12–13. *admit . . . service*] accept . . . as your lover.
19. *nice*] coy.

FOLLYWIT.

Why, I bind you by virtue of this chain to meet me tomorrow at the Flower-de-luce yonder, between nine and ten.

GUNWATER.

And if I do not, lady, let me lose it, thy love, and my best   25
fortunes.

FOLLYWIT.

Why now, I'll try you; go to!

GUNWATER.

Farewell, sweet lady.   *Kisses her. Exit.*

FOLLYWIT.

Welcome, sweet cockscomb; by my faith, a good induction. I
perceive by his overworn phrase, and his action toward the   30
middle region, still there has been some saucy nibbling
motion, and no doubt the cunning quean waited but for her
prey; and I think 'tis better bestow'd upon me for his soul's
health, and his body's, too. I'll teach the slave to be so bold
yet as once to offer to vault into his master's saddle, i' faith.   35
Now, casket, by your leave; I have seen your outside oft, but
that's no proof; some have fair outsides that are nothing
worth. Ha! Now, by my faith, a gentlewoman of very good
parts; diamond, ruby, saphire, *onyx cum prole silexque.* If I do
not wonder how the quean 'scap'd tempting, I'm an   40
hermaphrodite! Sure she could lack nothing but the devil
to point to't, and I wonder that he should be missing. Well,
'tis better as it is; this is the fruit of old grunting venery.
Grandsire, you may thank your drab for this; oh fie, in
your crinkling days, grandsire, keep a courtesan to hinder   45
your grandchild! 'Tis against nature, i' faith, and I hope
you'll be weary on't. Now to my villains that lurk close
below.
Who keeps a harlot, tell him this from me,
He needs nor thief, disease, nor enemy.   *Exit.* 50

---

24. ten] *Q1*; ten of the clocke *Q2*.   43. fruit] *Q1*; fruites *Q2*.
35. into] *Q1*; in *Q2*.

---

24. *Flower-de-luce*] a tavern.
39. *onyx . . . silexque*] "onyx (fingernail) with its compounds and silex
(flint)." Eberle identified this as part of a mnemonic quatrain in Lily's
Latin grammar, *Brevissima Institutio*, "The third Exception of Nouns
increasing short, being the Doubtfull Gender."

Enter Sir Bounteous.

SIR BOUNTEOUS.

Ah, sirrah, methink I feel myself well toasted, bumbasted,
rubb'd, and refresh'd. But i' faith, I cannot forget to think
how soon sickness has altered her to my taste. I gave her a
kiss at bottom o'th' stairs, and by th' mass, methought her
breath had much ado to be sweet, like a thing compounded,   55
methought, of wine, beer, and tobacco. I smelt much
pudding in't.
It may be but my fancy, or her physic;
For this I know, her health gave such content,
The fault rests in her sickness, or my scent.   60
How dost thou now, sweet girl; what, well recover'd?
Sickness quite gone, ha? Speak! Ha? Wench? Frank
Gullman! Why, body of me, what's here? My casket wide
open, broke open, my jewels stol'n! Why, Gunwater!

GUNWATER [*within*].

Anon, anon, sir.   65

SIR BOUNTEOUS.

Come hither, Gunwater.

GUNWATER [*within*].

That were small manners, sir, i' faith; I'll find a time anon.
Your worship's busy yet.

SIR BOUNTEOUS.

Why, Gunwater!

GUNWATER [*within*].

Foh, nay then, you'll make me blush, i' faith, sir.   70

[*Enter* Gunwater.]

SIR BOUNTEOUS.

Where's this creature?

GUNWATER.

What creature is't you'd have, sir?

SIR BOUNTEOUS.

The worst that ever breathes.

51. methink] *Q1*; methinkes *Q2*.

---

51. *sirrah*] Sir Bounteous presumably thinks Gunwater is in the room.
51. *bumbasted*] thrashed, with a pun on *bombasted*, "stuffed."
57. *pudding*] "A sort of tobacco (compressed into a solid shape, I suppose)"
(Bullen).

GUNWATER.

 , That's a wild boar, sir.

SIR BOUNTEOUS.

 That's a vild whore, sir. Where didst thou leave her, 75
rascal?

GUNWATER.

 Who, your recreation, sir?

SIR BOUNTEOUS.

 My execration, sir!

GUNWATER.

 Where I was wont, in your worship's closet.

SIR BOUNTEOUS.

 A pox engross her, it appears too true. See you this casket, 80
sir?

GUNWATER.

 My chain, my chain, my chain, my one and only chain! *Exit.*

SIR BOUNTEOUS.

 Thou run'st to much purpose now, Gunwater, yea? Is not a
quean enough to answer for, but she must join a thief to't?
A thieving quean! Nay, I have done with her, i' faith, 'tis a 85
sign sh'as been sick o' late, for she's a great deal worse than
she was. By my troth, I would have pawn'd my life upon't.
Did she want anything? Was she not supplied?
Nay, and liberally, for that's an old man's sin;
We'll feast our lechery though we starve our kin. 90
Is not my name Sir Bounteous? Am I not express'd there?
Ah, fie, fie, fie, fie, fie, but I perceive
Though she have never so complete a friend,
A strumpet's love will have a waft i'th' end
And distaste the vessel. I can hardly bear this. 95
But say I should complain, perhaps she has pawn'd 'em.
'Sfoot, the judges will but laugh at it, and bid her borrow
more money of 'em. Make the old fellow pay for's lechery,
that's all the mends I get. I have seen the same case tried at
Newbury the last 'sizes. Well, things must slip and sleep; I 100
will dissemble it

---

83. yea] *Dyce*; yee *Q1*.   83–84. Is . . . for] *one line in Q1.*

75. *vild*] vile.
94. *waft*] ill taste.
100. *'sizes*] assizes, the periodical county high court sessions.

Because my credit shall not lose her luster;
But whilst I live I'll neither love nor trust her.
I ha' done, I ha' done, I ha' done with her, i' faith.   *Exit.*

[IV.iv]   Master Penitent Brothel *knocking within; enter a* Servant.

SERVANT.
Who's that knocks?
PENITENT [*within*].
A friend.

Enter Master Penitent.

SERVANT.
What's your will, sir?
PENITENT.
Is Master Harebrain at home?
SERVANT.
No, newly gone from it, sir.   5
PENITENT.
Where's the gentlewoman his wife?
SERVANT.
My mistress is within, sir.
PENITENT.
When came she in, I pray?
SERVANT.
Who, my mistress? She was not out these two days to my
knowledge.   10
PENITENT.
No? Trust me, I'd thought I'd seen her. I would request a
word with her.
SERVANT.
I'll tell her, sir.   [*Exit.*]
PENITENT.
I thank you. —It likes me worse and worse.

Enter Mistress Harebrain.

MISTRESS HAREBRAIN.
Why, how now, sir? 'Twas desperately adventur'd; I   15

0.1. Brothel] *Once-Ill Q 1–2.*
0.1. Servant] *Seruus Q 1–2 (so through-
out scene in both quarto texts).*

2.1.] *after 0.1 in Q 1–2.*
4, 14.1, 50, 69.1. Harebrain] Hargraue *Q 1–2.*

little look'd for you until the morrow.

PENITENT.

No? Why, what made you at my chamber then even now?

MISTRESS HAREBRAIN.

I, at your chamber?

PENITENT.

Puh, dissemble not; come, come, you were there.

MISTRESS HAREBRAIN.

By my life, you wrong me, sir.   20

PENITENT.

What?

MISTRESS HAREBRAIN.

First, y'are not ignorant what watch keeps o'er me;
And for your chamber, as I live I know't not.

PENITENT.

Burst into sorrow then, and grief's extremes,
Whilst I beat on this flesh!

MISTRESS HAREBRAIN.   What is't disturbs you, sir?   25

PENITENT.

Then was the devil in your likeness there.

MISTRESS HAREBRAIN.

Ha?

PENITENT.

The very devil assum'd thee formally,
That face, that voice, that gesture, that attire,
E'en as it sits on thee, not a pleat alter'd,   30
That beaver band, the color of that periwig,
The farthingale above the navel, all,
As if the fashion were his own invention.

MISTRESS HAREBRAIN.

Mercy defend me!

PENITENT.   To beguile me more,
The cunning succubus told me that meeting   35

23. know't] *Q1*; know *Q2*.

---

17. *what . . . you*] what were you doing?
28. *assum'd . . . formally*] took your form.
31. *beaver band*] beaver-skin hat band.
32. *farthingale*] "stiff accessories used to hold out the skirts of women's
kirtles" (Linthicum, p. 179).

Was wrought o' purpose by much wit and art,
Wept to me, laid my vows before me, urg'd me,
Gave me the private marks of all our love,
Woo'd me in wanton and effeminate rhymes,
And sung and danc'd about me like a fairy;   40
And had not worthier cogitations bless'd me,
Thy form and his enchantments had possess'd me.

MISTRESS HAREBRAIN.

What shall become of me? My own thoughts doom me!

PENITENT.

Be honest; then the devil will ne'er assume thee.
He has no pleasure in that shape to abide   45
Where these two sisters reign not, lust or pride.
He as much trembles at a constant mind
As looser flesh at him. Be not dismay'd;
Spring souls for joy, his policies are betray'd.
Forgive me, Mistress Harebrain, on whose soul   50
The guilt hangs double,
My lust and thy enticement; both I challenge,
And therefore of due vengeance it appear'd
To none but me, to whom both sins inher'd.
What knows the lecher when he clips his whore   55
Whether it be the devil his parts adore?
They're both so like that, in our natural sense,
I could discern no change nor difference.
No marvel then times should so stretch and turn;
None for religion, all for pleasure burn.   60
Hot zeal into hot lust is now transform'd,
Grace into painting, charity into clothes,
Faith into false hair, and put off as often.
There's nothing but our virtue knows a mean;
He that kept open house now keeps a quean.   65
He will keep open still that he commends,
And there he keeps a table for his friends;

---

63. false] *Q1; not in Q2.*

---

49. *Spring souls*] Let souls spring.
50. *whose*] i.e., Penitent's.
52. *challenge*] claim.
66. *that*] that which.

And she consumes more than his sire could hoard,
Being more common than his house or board.

Enter Harebrain [*unnoticed*].

Live honest, and live happy, keep thy vows;   70
She's part a virgin whom but one man knows.
Embrace thy husband, and beside him none;
Having but one heart, give it but to one.

MISTRESS HAREBRAIN.

I vow it on my knees, with tears true bred,
No man shall ever wrong my husband's bed.   75

PENITENT.

Rise, I'm thy friend forever.

HAREBRAIN [*comes forward*].

And I thine forever and ever. Let me embrace thee, sir, whom
I will love even next unto my soul, and that's my wife;
Two dear rare gems this hour presents me with,
A wife that's modest, and a friend that's right.   80
Idle suspect and fear, now take your flight.

PENITENT.

A happy inward peace crown both your joys.

HAREBRAIN.

Thanks above utterance to you.

[*Enter* Servant.]

Now, the news?

SERVANT.

Sir Bounteous Progress, sir,
Invites you and my mistress to a feast   85
On Tuesday next; his man attends without.

HAREBRAIN.

Return both with our willingness and thanks.   [*Exit* Servant.]
I will entreat you, sir, to be my guest.

PENITENT.

Who, I, sir?

HAREBRAIN.

Faith, you shall.

68. his] *Dyce;* her *Q1–2.*   . . . thine/ For . . . will/ loue . . . wife
77–78. And . . . wife] *this edn.;* And   *Q1–2.*

-76-

PENITENT.   Well, I'll break strife.

HAREBRAIN.

   A friend's so rare, I'll sooner part from life.   [*Exeunt.*] 90

[IV.v]   *Enter* Follywit, *the* Courtesan *striving from him.*

FOLLYWIT.

   What, so coy, so strict? Come, come.

COURTESAN.

   Pray change your opinion, sir; I am not for that use.

FOLLYWIT.

   Will you but hear me?

COURTESAN.

   I shall hear that I would not.   *Exit.*

FOLLYWIT.

   'Sfoot, this is strange. I've seldom seen a wench stand   5
upon stricter points; life, she will not endure to be courted.
Does she e'er think to prosper? I'll ne'er believe that tree
can bring forth fruit that never bears a blossom; courtship's
a blossom, and often brings forth fruit in forty weeks. 'Twere
a mad part in me now to turn over; if ever there were any   10
hope on't, 'tis at this instant. Shall I be madder now than
ever I have been? I'm in the way, i' faith.
Man's never at high height of madness full
Until he love and prove a woman's gull.
I do protest in earnest I ne'er knew   15
At which end to begin to affect a woman
Till this bewitching minute; I ne'er saw
Face worth my object till mine eye met hers.
I should laugh and I were caught, i' faith; I'll see her again,
that's certain, whate'er comes on't—by your favor, ladies.   20

Enter the Mother.

90. S.P. HAREBRAIN] *Harg. Q1–2.*   19. I . . . laugh] *Dyce; part of l.18*
[IV.v]   *in Q1–2.*
18. Face] *Q1;* Each *Q2.*

---

12. *in*] on.
20. *by . . . ladies*] Addressed to the audience.

4+

MOTHER.

You're welcome, sir.

FOLLYWIT.

Know you the young gentlewoman that went in lately?

MOTHER.

I have best cause to know her; I'm her mother, sir.

FOLLYWIT.

Oh, in good time. I like the gentlewoman well; a pretty, contriv'd beauty.   25

MOTHER.

Ay, nature has done her part, sir.

FOLLYWIT.

But she has one uncomely quality.

MOTHER.

What's that, sir?

FOLLYWIT.

'Sfoot, she's afraid of a man.

MOTHER.

Alas, impute that to her bashful spirit; she's fearful of her   30
honor.

FOLLYWIT.

Of her honor? 'Slid, I'm sure I cannot get her maidenhead with breathing upon her, nor can she lose her honor in her tongue.

MOTHER.

True, and I have often told her so. But what would you have   35
of a foolish virgin, sir, a wilful virgin? I tell you, sir, I need
not have been in that solitary estate that I am, had she had
grace and boldness to have put herself forward. Always
timorsome, always backward; ah, that same peevish honor
of hers has undone her and me both, good gentleman. The   40
suitors, the jewels, the jointures that has been offer'd her!
We had been made women forever, but what was her
fashion? She could not endure the sight of a man, forsooth,
but run and hole herself presently. So choice of her honor, I
am persuaded whene'er she has husband   45

36. of] *Q1; not in Q2.*

---

39. *peevish*] foolish.

She will e'en be a precedent for all married wives,
How to direct their actions and their lives.

FOLLYWIT.

Have you not so much power with her to command her
presence?

MOTHER.

You shall see straight what I can do, sir.   *Exit.* 50

FOLLYWIT.

Would I might be hang'd if my love do not stretch to her
deeper and deeper; those bashful maiden humors take me
prisoner. When there comes a restraint on't, upon flesh, we
are always most greedy upon't, and that makes your
merchant's wife oftentimes pay so dear for a mouthful. Give 55
me a woman as she was made at first, simple of herself, without sophistication like this wench; I cannot abide them when
they have tricks, set speeches, and artful entertainments. You
shall have some so impudently aspected they will outcry the
forehead of a man, make him blush first, and talk him into 60
silence, and this is counted manly in a woman. It may hold
so; sure, womanly it is not; no,
If e'er I love, or anything move me,
'Twill be a woman's simple modesty.

Enter Mother *bringing in strivingly the* Courtesan.

COURTESAN.

Pray let me go; why, mother, what do you mean? I 65
beseech you, mother! Is this your conquest now? Great
glory 'tis to overcome a poor and silly virgin.

FOLLYWIT.

The wonder of our time sits in that brow;
I ne'er beheld a perfect maid till now.

MOTHER.

Thou childish thing, more bashful than thou'rt wise,   70
Why dost thou turn aside and drown thine eyes?

46–47. She . . . lives] *Dyce; prose in*   53. on't] *Q1; not in Q2.*
Q1–2.   69. maid] *Dyce;* man *Q1–2*

53–55. *When . . . mouthful*] an allusion to paying black market prices for
meat forbidden to be sold during Lent.
  67. *silly*] defenceless.

–79–

Look, fearful fool, there's no temptation near thee;
Art not asham'd that any flesh should fear thee?
Why, I durst pawn my life the gentleman means no other
but honest and pure love to thee. How say you, sir?   75

FOLLYWIT.

By my faith, not I, lady.

MOTHER.

Hark you there? What think you now, forsooth? What
grieves your honor now?
Or what lascivious breath intends to rear
Against that maiden organ, your chaste ear?   80
Are you resolv'd now better of men's hearts,
Their faiths, and their affections? With you none,
Or at most few, whose tongues and minds are one.
Repent you now of your opinion past;
Men love as purely as you can be chaste.   85
To her yourself, sir, the way's broke before you;
You have the easier passage.

FOLLYWIT.   Fear not; come,
Erect thy happy graces in thy look.
I am no curious wooer, but, in faith,
I love thee honorably.

COURTESAN.   How mean you that, sir?   90

FOLLYWIT.

'Sfoot, as one loves a woman for a wife.

MOTHER.

Has the gentleman answered you, trow?

FOLLYWIT.

I do confess it truly to you both,
My estate is yet but sickly; but I've a grandsire
Will make me lord of thousands at his death.   95

MOTHER.

I know your grandsire well; she knows him better.

86–88. To . . . look] *Dyce;* to . . .
sir/ The . . . passage/ Feare . . . looke
Q1–2.
89. am] *Q1;* love *Q2.*

89. curious] *Q1 (corr.);* urious *Q1
(uncorr.).*
92. gentleman] *Q1;* gentlemen *Q2.*

73. *fear*] frighten.
82. *you none*] i.e., there are none.
92. *trow*] do you believe?

FOLLYWIT.

Why then, you know no fiction. My state then
Will be a long day's journey 'bove the waste, wench.

MOTHER.

Nay, daughter, he says true.

FOLLYWIT.

And thou shalt often measure it in thy coach,   100
And with the wheels' track make a girdle for't.

MOTHER.

Ah, 'twill be a merry journey.

FOLLYWIT.

What, is't a match? If't be, clap hands and lips.

MOTHER.

'Tis done, there's witness on't.

FOLLYWIT.

Why then, mother, I salute you.   105

MOTHER.

Thanks, sweet son. Son Follywit, come hither; if I might
counsel thee, we'll e'en take her while the good mood's
upon her. Send for a priest and clap't up within this hour.

FOLLYWIT.

By my troth, agreed, mother.

MOTHER.

Nor does her wealth consist all in her flesh,   110
Though beauty be enough wealth for a woman;
She brings a dowry of three hundred pound with her.

FOLLYWIT.

'Sfoot, that will serve till my grandsire dies; I warrant you
he'll drop away at fall o'th' leaf. If ever he reach to All
Hollandtide, I'll be hang'd.   115

97–98.] *Dyce; prose in Q1–2.*   112. pound] *Q1; not in Q2.*
99. Nay] *Q1;* My *Q2.*

_____

97. *state*] estate.
98. *waste*] unproductive land.
104. *witness*] The mother witnesses a binding betrothal, legally a marriage
but requiring solemnization before a priest. Follywit is thus justified in
calling the bawd "mother."
114–115. *All Hollandtide*] the season of the feast of All Saints, November 1.

MOTHER.

Oh yes, son, he's a lusty old gentleman.

FOLLYWIT.

Ah, pox, he's given to women; he keeps a quean at this
present.

MOTHER.

Fie!

FOLLYWIT.

Do not tell my wife on't.   120

MOTHER.

That were needless, i' faith.

FOLLYWIT.

He makes a great feast upon the 'leventh of this month,
Tuesday next, and you shall see players there.—[*Aside.*] I
have one trick more to put upon him.—My wife and yourself
shall go thither before as my guests, and prove his enter- 125
tainment; I'll meet you there at night. The jest will be here:
that feast which he makes will, unknown to him, serve fitly
for our wedding dinner. We shall be royally furnish'd, and
get some charges by't.

MOTHER.

An excellent course, i' faith, and a thrifty. Why, son,   130
methinks you begin to thrive before y'are married.

FOLLYWIT.

We shall thrive one day, wench, and clip enough;
Between our hopes there's but a grandsire's puff.   *Exit.*

MOTHER.

So, girl, here was a bird well caught.

COURTESAN.

If ever, here;   135
But what for's grandsire? 'Twill scarce please him well.

MOTHER.

Who covets fruit, ne'er cares from whence it fell;
Thou'st wedded youth and strength, and wealth will fall.
Last, thou'rt made honest.

---

131. methinks] *Q1*; me thinke *Q2*.   135–136.] *Dyce; prose in Q1–2.*

---

129. *charges*] profit (?)
132. *and clip*] if we embrace. Eberle suspects a triple pun: "embrace,"
"seize," and "dishonestly scrape gold off the edges of coins."

COURTESAN.   And that's worth 'em all.   *Exeunt.*

[*Finit Actus Quartus.*]

[V.i]   [*Incipit*] *Actus Quintus: Ultimus*
Enter busily Sir Bounteous Progress, [Gunwater, *servants*] *for the feast.*

SIR BOUNTEOUS.
    Have a care, blue coats. Bestir yourself, Master Gunwater,
    cast an eye into th' kitchen, o'erlook the knaves a little.
    Every jack has his friend today, this cousin and that cousin
    puts in for a dish of meat; a man knows not till he make a
    feast how many varlets he feeds; acquaintances swarm in   5
    every corner like flies at Barthol'mew-tide that come up with
    drovers. 'Sfoot, I think they smell my kitchen seven mile
    about.

        [*Enter* Harebrain, Mistress Harebrain, Penitent Brothel.]

    Master Harebrain and his sweet bedfellow, y'are very copi-
    ously welcome.   10
HAREBRAIN.
    Sir, here's an especial dear friend of ours; we were bold to
    make his way to your table.
SIR BOUNTEOUS.
    Thanks for that boldness ever, good Master Harebrain. Is
    this your friend, sir?
HAREBRAIN.
    Both my wife's friend and mine, sir.   15
SIR BOUNTEOUS.
    Why then compendiously, sir, y'are welcome.
PENITENT.
    In octavo I thank you, sir.
SIR BOUNTEOUS.
    Excellently retorted, i' faith; he's welcome for's wit. I have

0.1. *Ultimus*] *Vlli Q1.*   9, 13. Harebrain] *Shortrod Q1–2 (see*
                                        Intro., p. xviii).

---

    1. *blue coats*] see I.i.73.n.   2. *knaves*] servants.
    6. *Barthol'mew-tide*] August 24, the time of the annual fair held in the
suburb of Smithfield.

my sorts of salutes, and know how to place 'em courtly.
Walk in, sweet gentlemen, walk in, there's a good fire i'th'   20
hall. You shall have my sweet company instantly.

HAREBRAIN.

Ay, good Sir Bounteous.

SIR BOUNTEOUS.

You shall indeed, gentlemen.   [*Exeunt* Harebrains, Penitent.]

Enter Servant.

How now, what news brings thee in stumbling now?

SERVANT.

There are certain players come to town, sir, and desire to   25
interlude before your worship.

SIR BOUNTEOUS.

Players? By the mass, they are welcome; they'll grace my
entertainment well. But for certain players, there thou liest,
boy; they were never more uncertain in their lives. Now up
and now down, they know not when to play, where to play,   30
nor what to play; not when to play for fearful fools, where
to play for Puritan fools, nor what to play for critical
fools. Go, call 'em in.   [*Exit* Servant.]
How fitly the whoresons come upo'th' feast; troth, I was
e'en wishing for 'em.   35

[*Re-enter* Servant *with* Follywit, Mawworm, Hoboy *and others disguised
as players.*]

Oh, welcome, welcome, my friends!

FOLLYWIT.

The month of May delights not in her flowers
More than we joy in that sweet sight of yours.

SIR BOUNTEOUS.

Well acted, o' my credit; I perceive he's your best actor.

SERVANT.

He has greatest share, sir, and may live of himself, sir.   40

23.1. S.D.] *after l. 22 in Q 1–2*.   25, 40. S.P. SERVANT] *Semus Q 1–*
23.1. Servant] *Semus Q 1–2*.   (*probably a misreading of "Seruus";
                                        see Intro., p. xviii*).

25–26. *to interlude*] to act, usually in the intervals of a festivity.
31. *fearful fools*] i.e., fearful about the plague. When plague deaths
reached a certain number per week, the theaters were closed.
40. *He . . . share*] owns the most shares in the players' stock company.

SIR BOUNTEOUS.

What, what? Put on your hat, sir, pray put on! Go to, wealth
must be respected; let those that have least feathers stand
bare. And whose men are you, I pray? Nay, keep on your
hat still.

FOLLYWIT.

We serve my Lord Owemuch, sir.   45

SIR BOUNTEOUS.

My Lord Owemuch? By my troth, the welcom'st men alive!
Give me all your hands at once. That honorable gentleman?
He lay at my house in a robbery once, and took all quietly,
went cheerfully. I made a very good feast for him. I never
saw a man of honor bear things bravelier away. Serve my   50
Lord Owemuch? Welcome, i' faith. Some bastard for my
lord's players!   [*Exit* Servant.]
Where be your boys?

FOLLYWIT.

They come along with the wagon, sir.

SIR BOUNTEOUS.

Good, good; and which is your politician amongst you?   55
Now, i' faith, he that works out restraints, makes best legs at
court, and has a suit made of purpose for the company's
business, which is he? Come, be not afraid of him.

FOLLYWIT.

I am he, sir.

SIR BOUNTEOUS.

Art thou he? Give me thy hand. Hark in thine ear; thou   60
rollest too fast to gather so much moss as thy fellow there;
champ upon that. Ah, and what play shall we have, my
masters?

FOLLYWIT.

A pleasant witty comedy, sir.

41. pray put] *Q1*; pray goe *Q2*.   63. masters] *Q1* (*corr.*); masterssts
53. your] *Q2*; you *Q1*.   *Q1* (*uncorr.*).

42. *feathers*] plumes in actors' hats.
55–58. *politician . . . business*] Eberle suggests that this refers to the
actor John Heminges, one of the King's Men who apparently functioned as
business agent for the company (see Chambers, II, 321). "Restraints" were
prohibitions from acting, as during Lent or plague-time.
58. *of*] for.

SIR BOUNTEOUS.

Ay, ay, ay, a comedy in any case, that I and my guests may   65
laugh a little. What's the name on't?

FOLLYWIT.

'Tis call'd *The Slip*.

SIR BOUNTEOUS.

The Slip? By my troth, a pretty name, and a glib one! Go all,
and slip into't as fast as you can.—Cover a table for the
players!—First take heed of a lurcher; he cuts deep, he will   70
eat up all from you.—Some sherry for my lord's players
there, sirrah!—Why, this will be a true feast, a right Miter
supper, a play, and all.

                              [*Exeunt* Follywit *and the others.*]

More lights!

              Enter Mother *and* Courtesan.

I call'd for light; here come in two are light enough for a   75
whole house, i' faith. Dare the thief look me i'th' face? Oh
impudent times! Go to, dissemble it!

MOTHER.

Bless you, Sir Bounteous!

SIR BOUNTEOUS.

Oh, welcome, welcome, thief, quean, and bawd, welcome
all three!   80

MOTHER.

Nay, here's but two on's, sir.

SIR BOUNTEOUS.

O' my troth, I took her for a couple; I'd have sworn there
had been two faces there.

MOTHER.

Not all under one hood, sir.

---

70. lurcher] *Q1* (*corr.*); Lurchir *Q1*   (*uncorr.*).
(*uncorr.*).   74.1.] *after l. 77 Q1* (*corr.*)*; not in Q1*
72. Miter] *Q1* (*corr.*); Niter *Q1*   (*uncorr.*).

    67. *The Slip*] A slip was a counterfeit coin.
    70. *lurcher*] "One who . . . forestalls others of their fair share of food"
(*OED*); but also "swindler, rogue."
    72. *Miter*] a tavern which Middleton elsewhere (*Your Five Gallants*,
II.i.216) prefers over Jonson's Mermaid.

SIR BOUNTEOUS.

    Yes, faith, would I, to see mine eyes bear double.   85

MOTHER.

    I'll make it hold, sir, my daughter is a couple. She was
married yesterday.

SIR BOUNTEOUS.

    Buz!

MOTHER.

    Nay, to no buzzard neither; a right hawk
Whene'er you know him.   90

SIR BOUNTEOUS.

    Away! He cannot be but a rascal.
Walk in, walk in, bold guests that come unsent for.

                                 [*Exit* Mother.]

    Pox, I perceive how my jewels went now:
To grace her marriage.

COURTESAN.

                Would you with me, sir?

SIR BOUNTEOUS.

    Ay; how happ'd it, wench, you put the slip upon me   95
Not three nights since? I name it gently to you;
I term it neither pilfer, cheat, nor shark.

COURTESAN.

    Y'are past my reach.

SIR BOUNTEOUS.

    I'm old and past your reach, very good; but you will not
deny this, I trust.   100

COURTESAN.

    With a safe conscience, sir.

SIR BOUNTEOUS.

    Yea? Give me thy hand; fare thee well. I have done with
her.

---

88. Buz] *Q1* (*corr.*); Buzy *Q1*
(*uncorr.*).
91–94. Away . . . marriage] *Dyce;*
prose in Q1–2.
93. Pox] *Dyce*; Post *Q1–2.*
97. pilfer] *Q1* (*corr.*); Gilfer *Q1*

(*uncorr.*).
102. Yea] *Dyce*; Yee *Q1.*
102. thee] *Q1* (*corr.*); him *Q1*
(*uncorr.*).
103. her] *Q1* (*corr.*); him *Q1*
(*uncorr.*).

---

94. *Would . . . me*] What do you want with me?
97. *pilfer . . . shark*] theft.

COURTESAN.

    Give me your hand, sir; you ne'er yet begun with me.   *Exit.*

SIR BOUNTEOUS.

    Whew, whew! Oh, audacious age!   105
    She denies me and all, when on her fingers
    I spied the ruby sit that does betray her
    And blushes for her face. Well, there's a time for't,
    For all's too little now for entertainment,
    Feast, mirth, ay, harmony, and the play to boot: 110
    A jovial season.

                  Enter Follywit.

            How now, are you ready?

FOLLYWIT.

    Even upon readiness, sir.   *Takes hat off.*

SIR BOUNTEOUS.

    Keep you your hat on.

FOLLYWIT.

    I have a suit to your worship.

SIR BOUNTEOUS.

    Oh, cry you mercy; then you must stand bare.   115

FOLLYWIT.

    We could do all to the life of action, sir, both for the credit
    of your worship's house and the grace of our comedy—

SIR BOUNTEOUS.

    Cuds me, what else, sir?

FOLLYWIT.

    And for some defects, as the custom is, we would be bold to
    require your worship's assistance.   120

SIR BOUNTEOUS.

    Why, with all my heart; what is't you want? Speak.

FOLLYWIT.

    One's a chain for a justice's hat, sir.

SIR BOUNTEOUS.

    Why, here, here, here, here, whoreson, will this serve your
    turn? What else lack you?

105. Whew, whew] *Q1* (*corr.*);
When, when *Q1* (*uncorr.*).
107. sit] *Q1* (*corr.*); sir *Q1* (*uncorr.*).
108. face] *this edn.*; fact *Q1–2*.

112. S.D. *hat*] *it Q1–2* (*where S.D. is
printed on l. 113*).
124. turn? What] *this edn.*; turn?
Sir Bo. What *Q1*; turn? *Fol*.
Excellent well sir. *Q2*.

FOLLYWIT.
    We should use a ring with a stone in't.   125
SIR BOUNTEOUS.
    Nay, whoop, I have given too many rings already; talk no
    more of rings, I pray you. Here, here, here, make this jewel
    serve for once.
FOLLYWIT.
    Oh, this will serve, sir.
SIR BOUNTEOUS.
    What, have you all now?   130
FOLLYWIT.
    All now, sir. Only Time is brought i'th' middle of the play,
    and I would desire your worship's watch.
SIR BOUNTEOUS.
    My watch? With all my heart; only give Time a charge
    that he be not fiddling with it.
FOLLYWIT.
    You shall ne'er see that, sir.   135
SIR BOUNTEOUS.
    Well, now you are furnish'd, sir, make haste, away.
                                                    [*Exit.*]

FOLLYWIT.
    E'en as fast as I can, sir. I'll set my fellows going first; they
    must have time and leisure, or they're dull else. I'll stay and
    speak a prologue, yet o'ertake 'em; I cannot have conscience,
    i' faith, to go away and speak ne'er a word to 'em. My   140
    grandsire has given me three shares here; sure I'll do
    somewhat for 'em.   *Exit.*

[V.ii]
Enter Sir Bounteous and all the guests [Harebrain, Mistress Harebrain,
Penitent Brothel, Frank Gullman *and her Mother, and other guests*:
Gunwater *and servants*].

SIR BOUNTEOUS.
    More lights! More stools! Sit, sit, the play begins.
HAREBRAIN.
    Have you players here, Sir Bounteous?

132. watch] *this edn.*; watch time   [V.ii]
Q1–2.   2. S.P. HAREBRAIN] *Short. Q1–2 (so*
140. speak] *Q1; not in Q2.*   *to end of both quarto texts*).

SIR BOUNTEOUS.

We have 'em for you, sir; fine, nimble comedians, proper
actors, most of them.

PENITENT.

Whose men, I pray you, sir?   5

SIR BOUNTEOUS.

Oh, there's their credit, sir; they serve an honorable
popular gentleman yclipped my Lord Owemuch.

HAREBRAIN.

My Lord Owemuch? He was in Ireland lately.

SIR BOUNTEOUS.

Oh, you ne'er knew any of the name but were great
travelers.   10

HAREBRAIN.

How is the comedy call'd, Sir Bounteous?

SIR BOUNTEOUS.

Marry, sir, *The Slip*.

HAREBRAIN.

The Slip?

SIR BOUNTEOUS.

Ay, and here's the Prologue begins to slip in upon's.

HAREBRAIN.

'Tis so indeed, Sir Bounteous.   15

Enter, for a Prologue, Follywit.

Prologue

FOLLYWIT.

We sing of wand'ring knights, what them betide
Who nor in one place nor one shape abide;
They're here now, and anon no scouts can reach 'em,
Being every man well-hors'd like a bold Beacham.
The play which we present no fault shall meet   20
But one: you'll say 'tis short, we'll say 'tis sweet.
'Tis given much to dumb shows, which some praise,
And like the Term, delights much in delays.

3. fine] *Q1*; five *Q2*.

---

7. *yclipped*] named.

19. *bold Beacham*] "'As bold as Beauchamp' is an old proverb founded on
the exploits of Thomas, first Earl of Warwick" (Bullen).

22. *dumb shows*] pantomimes forming part of the action of a play.

23. *Term*] law term, the time in which court is held.

So to conclude, and give the name her due,
The play being call'd "The Slip," I vanish too.   *Exit.* 25

SIR BOUNTEOUS.

Excellently well acted, and a nimble conceit.

HAREBRAIN.

The Prologue's pretty, i' faith.

PENITENT.

And went off well.

SIR BOUNTEOUS.

Ay, that's the grace of all, when they go away well, ah!

COURTESAN.

O' my troth, and I were not married I could find in my   30
heart to fall in love with that player now, and send for him to
a supper. I know some i' th' town that have done as much, and
there took such a good conceit of their parts into th' two-
penny room that the actors have been found i' th' morning
in a less compass than their stage, though 'twere ne'er so full   35
of gentlemen.

SIR BOUNTEOUS.

But, passion of me, where be these knaves? Will they not
come away? Methinks they stay very long.

PENITENT.

Oh, you must bear a little, sir; they have many shifts to run
into.   40

SIR BOUNTEOUS.

Shifts call you 'em? They're horrible long things.

Followit *returns in a fury.*

FOLLYWIT [*aside*].

A pox of such fortune! The plot's betray'd! All will come out;
yonder they come, taken upon suspicion and brought back
by a constable. I was accurs'd to hold society with such

29. ah] *Q1*; ah, ah *Q2*.   41.1.] *after "betray'd" (l. 42) in Q1.*

26. *nimble conceit*] lively invention.
30–36.] It was apparently common for prostitutes to sup with players at
the theater after a play.
35–36. *stage . . . gentlemen*] alluding to the practice of gallants sitting on
stage during a performance.
39. *shifts*] changes of costume.

cockscombs! What's to be done? I shall be sham'd forever,   45
my wife here and all. Ah, pox! By light, happily thought
upon: the chain! Invention, stick to me this once, and fail
me ever hereafter. So, so.

SIR BOUNTEOUS.

Life, I say, where be these players? Oh, are you come?
Troth, it's time; I was e'en sending for you.   50

HAREBRAIN.

How moodily he walks; what plays he, trow?

SIR BOUNTEOUS.

A justice, upon my credit; I know by the chain there.

FOLLYWIT.

Unfortunate justice!

SIR BOUNTEOUS.

Ah, a, a.

FOLLYWIT.

In thy kin unfortunate!   55
Here comes thy nephew now upon suspicion,
Brought by a constable before thee, his vild associates with him,
But so disguis'd none knows him but myself.
Twice have I set him free from officers' fangs,
And, for his sake, his fellows. Let him look to't;   60
My conscience will permit but one wink more.

SIR BOUNTEOUS.

Yea, shall we take justice winking?

FOLLYWIT.

For this time I have bethought a means to work thy freedom, though
hazarding myself; should the law seize him,
Being kin to me, 'twould blemish much my name.   65
No, I'd rather lean to danger than to shame.

Enter Constable *with them* [Mawworm, Hoboy, *and others*].

SIR BOUNTEOUS.

A very explete justice.

---

52. A justice] A, Iustice *Q1 (corr.)*;   60. *Let him*] *Q1; not in Q2.*
Ha, Iustice *Q1 (uncorr.).*   62. Yea] *Dyce;* Yee *Q1.*

---

67. *explete*] complete, perfect.

CONSTABLE.
  Thank you, good neighbors; let me alone with 'em now.

MAWWORM.
  'Sfoot, who's yonder?

HOBOY.
  Dare he sit there?   70

SECOND.
  Follywit!

THIRD.
  Captain! Puh!

FOLLYWIT.
  How now, constable, what news with thee?

CONSTABLE.
  May it please your worship, sir, here are a company of
  auspicious fellows.   75

SIR BOUNTEOUS.
  To me? Puh! Turn to th' justice, you whoreson hobbyhorse!
  This is some new player now; they put all their fools to the
  constable's part still.

FOLLYWIT.
  What's the matter, constable, what's the matter?

CONSTABLE.
  I have nothing to say to your worship. —They were all   80
  riding a-horseback, an't please your worship.

SIR BOUNTEOUS.
  Yet again? A pox of all asses still! They could not ride afoot
  unless 'twere in a bawdy house.

CONSTABLE.
  The ostler told me they were all unstable fellows, sir.

FOLLYWIT.
  Why, sure the fellow's drunk!   85

MAWWORM.
  We spied that weakness in him long ago, sir. Your worship must
  bear with him; the man's much o'erseen. Only in respect of his

70. S.P. HOBOY] *Anc. Q1 (corr.);*
An.c Q1 (uncorr.).

---

75. *auspicious*] "suspicious," a typical comic malapropism.
87. *o'erseen*] "deceived," but also "drunk."

office we obey'd him, both to appear comfortable to law, and clear of
all offense. For I protest, sir, he found us but a-horseback.

FOLLYWIT.

    What, he did? 90

MAWWORM.

    As I have a soul, that's all, and all he can lay to us.

CONSTABLE.

    I' faith, you were not all riding away, then?

MAWWORM.

    'Sfoot, being a-horseback, sir, that must needs follow.

FOLLYWIT.

    Why true, sir.

SIR BOUNTEOUS.

    Well said, justice. He helps his kinsman well. 95

FOLLYWIT.

    Why, sirrah, do you use to bring gentlemen before us for riding
away? What, will you have 'em stand still when they're up, like
Smug upo'th' white horse yonder? Are your wits steep'd? I'll make
you an example for all dizzy constables! How they abuse justice!
Here, bind him to this chair. 100

CONSTABLE.

    Ha, bind him? Ho!

FOLLYWIT.

    If you want cords, use garters.

CONSTABLE.

    Help, help, gentlemen!

MAWWORM.

    As fast as we can, sir.

CONSTABLE.

    Thieves, thieves! 105

FOLLYWIT.

    A gag will help all this. Keep less noise, you knave!

---

95. kinsman] *Q1*; kinsmen *Q2*.
99. *example*] *Q1*; *excellent example*
Q2.

99. *dizzy*] *Q1 (corr.)*; *ditch Q1*
(uncorr.).
101. Ho] *Q1 (corr.)*; here *Q1*
(uncorr.).

---

98. *Smug . . . horse*] reference to a scene (missing from the extant version)
of *The Merry Devil of Edmonton* in which Smug plays St. George riding upon
a white horse.
102. *want*] lack.

CONSTABLE.

    Oh help, rescue the constable! Oh, oh!   [*They gag him.*]

SIR BOUNTEOUS.

    Ho, ho, ho, ho!

FOLLYWIT.

    Why, la you, who lets you now?
    You may ride quietly; I'll see you to   110
    Take horse myself. I have nothing else to do.
                Exeunt [Follywit, Mawworm, Hoboy, *and others*].

CONSTABLE.

    Oh, oh, oh!

SIR BOUNTEOUS.

    Ha, ha, ha! By my troth, the maddest piece of justice,
    gentlemen, that ever was committed!

HAREBRAIN.

    I'll be sworn for the madness on't, sir.   115

SIR BOUNTEOUS.

    I am deceiv'd if this prove not a merry comedy and a witty.

PENITENT.

    Alas, poor constable, his mouth's open and ne'er a wise word.

SIR BOUNTEOUS.

    Faith, he speaks now e'en as many as he has done; he seems
    wisest when he gapes and says nothing. Ha, ha, he turns and
    tells his tale to me like an ass. What have I to do with their 120
    riding away? They may ride for me, thou whoreson cocks-
    comb, thou; nay, thou art well enough serv'd, i' faith.

PENITENT.

    But what follows all this while, sir? Methinks some should
    pass by before this time and pity the constable.

SIR BOUNTEOUS.

    By th' mass, and you say true, sir. Go, sirrah, step in; I 125
    think they have forgot themselves. Call the knaves away;
    they're in a wood, I believe.   [*Exit* Servant.]

CONSTABLE.

    Ay, ay, ay!

---

107. S.D.] *Q2; not in Q1.*   115, 135, 139. S.P. HAREBRAIN]
111.1 *Exeunt*] *Dyce; Exit Q1.*   *Short. R. Q1 (corr.); Short. Q1*
                        (uncorr.).

---

  109. *lets*] hinders.

SIR BOUNTEOUS.

Hark, the constable says ay, they're in a wood! Ha, ha!

GUNWATER.

He thinks long of the time, Sir Bounteous.   130

[*Enter* Servant.]

SIR BOUNTEOUS.

How now? When come they?

SERVANT.

Alas, an't please your worship, there's not one of them to be
found, sir.

SIR BOUNTEOUS.

How?

HAREBRAIN.

What says the fellow?   135

SERVANT.

Neither horse nor man, sir.

SIR BOUNTEOUS.

Body of me, thou liest!

SERVANT.

Not a hair of either, sir.

HAREBRAIN.

How now, Sir Bounteous?

SIR BOUNTEOUS.

Cheated and defeated! Ungag that rascal; I'll hang him   140
for's fellows, I'll make him bring 'em out.

CONSTABLE.

Did not I tell your worship this before? Brought 'em before
you for suspected persons? Stay'd 'em at town's end upon
warning given? Made signs that my very jawbone aches?
Your worship would not hear me, call'd me ass, saving your   145
worship's presence, laugh'd at me.

SIR BOUNTEOUS.

Ha?

HAREBRAIN.

I begin to taste it.

130. S.P. GUNWATER] *Nub Q1;*
Gum Q2.

---

130. S.P. GUNWATER] Q1 *Nub* is meaningless, but may refer to a guest.

SIR BOUNTEOUS.

Give me leave, give me leave. Why, art not thou the
constable i'th' comedy?   150

CONSTABLE.

I'th' comedy? Why, I am the constable i'th' commonwealth,
sir.

SIR BOUNTEOUS.

I am gull'd, i' faith, I am gull'd! When wast thou chose?

CONSTABLE.

On Thursday last, sir.

SIR BOUNTEOUS.

A pox go with't, there't goes!   155

PENITENT.

I seldom heard jest match it.

HAREBRAIN.

Nor I, i' faith.

SIR BOUNTEOUS.

Gentlemen, shall I entreat a courtesy?

HAREBRAIN.

What is't, sir?

SIR BOUNTEOUS.

Do not laugh at me seven year hence.   160

PENITENT.

We should betray and laugh at our own folly then, for of
my troth none here but was deceiv'd in't.

SIR BOUNTEOUS.

Faith, that's some comfort yet. Ha, ha, it was featly carried!
Troth, I commend their wits! Before our faces make us
asses, while we sit still and only laugh at ourselves.   165

PENITENT.

Faith, they were some counterfeit rogues, sir.

SIR BOUNTEOUS.

Why, they confess so much themselves; they said they'd play
The Slip; they should be men of their words. I hope the
justice will have more conscience, i' faith, than to carry
away a chain of a hundred mark of that fashion.   170

---

156. heard] *Q1*; heard a *Q2*.   167. so much] *Q1*; as much *Q2*.
158. shall I] *Q1*; I shall *Q2*.

---

163. *featly*] deftly.
170. *mark*] a sum of money worth thirteen shillings fourpence.

HAREBRAIN.

What, sir?

SIR BOUNTEOUS.

Ay, by my troth, sir; besides a jewel and a jewel's fellow, a
good fair watch that hung about my neck, sir.

HAREBRAIN.

'Sfoot, what did you mean, sir?

SIR BOUNTEOUS.

Methinks my Lord Owemuch's players should not scorn me   175
so, i' faith; they will come and bring all again, I know. Push,
they will, i' faith; but a jest, certainly.

Enter Follywit *in his own shape, and all the rest* [Mawworm, Hoboy *and
others*].

FOLLYWIT.

Pray, grandsire, give me your blessing.

SIR BOUNTEOUS.

Who? Son Follywit?

FOLLYWIT [*aside*].

This shows like kneeling after the play, I praying for my   180
Lord Owemuch and his good countess, our honorable lady
and mistress.

SIR BOUNTEOUS.

Rise richer by a blessing; thou art welcome.

FOLLYWIT.

Thanks, good grandsire. I was bold to bring those gentlemen,
my friends.   185

SIR BOUNTEOUS.

They're all welcome. Salute you that side, and I'll welcome
this side. —Sir, to begin with you.

HAREBRAIN.

Master Follywit.

FOLLYWIT.

I am glad 'tis our fortune so happily to meet, sir.

---

180. *kneeling . . . play*] "A practice of offering up a prayer for the lord's
well-being at the end of a performance was probably of ancient derivation,
although whether it survived in the public theatres may perhaps be doubted"
(Chambers, I, 311).

186–187. *Salute . . . side*] Sir Bounteous and Follywit greet the assembled
company, each going to the group he does not know.

SIR BOUNTEOUS.

Nay, then you know me not, sir.   190

FOLLYWIT.

Sweet Mistress Harebrain.

SIR BOUNTEOUS.

You cannot be too bold, sir.

FOLLYWIT.

Our marriage known?

COURTESAN.

Not a word yet.

FOLLYWIT.

The better.   195

SIR BOUNTEOUS.

Faith, son, would you had come sooner with these gentlemen.

FOLLYWIT.

Why, grandsire?

SIR BOUNTEOUS.

We had a play here.

FOLLYWIT.

A play, sir? No.   200

SIR BOUNTEOUS.

Yes, faith, a pox o'th' author!

FOLLYWIT [aside].

Bless us all! —Why, were they such vild ones, sir?

SIR BOUNTEOUS.

I am sure villainous ones, sir.

FOLLYWIT.

Some raw, simple fools?

SIR BOUNTEOUS.

Nay, by th' mass, these were enough for thievish knaves.   205

FOLLYWIT.

What, sir?

SIR BOUNTEOUS.

Which way came you, gentlemen? You could not choose
but meet 'em.

FOLLYWIT.

We met a company with hampers after 'em.

SIR BOUNTEOUS.

Oh, those were they, those were they, a pox hamper 'em!   210

FOLLYWIT [aside].

Bless us all again!

SIR BOUNTEOUS.

They have hamper'd me finely, sirrah.

FOLLYWIT.

How, sir?

SIR BOUNTEOUS.

How, sir? I lent the rascals properties to furnish out their
play, a chain, a jewel, and a watch, and they watch'd their   215
time and rid quite away with 'em.

FOLLYWIT.

Are they such creatures?

SIR BOUNTEOUS.

Hark, hark, gentlemen! By this light, the watch rings
alarum in his pocket! There's my watch come again, or the
very cousin-german to't. Whose is't, whose is't? By th' mass,   220
'tis he; hast thou one, son? Prithee bestow it upon thy
grandsire. I now look for mine again, i' faith. Nay, come with
a good will or not at all; I'll give thee a better thing. A
prize, a prize, gentlemen!

HAREBRAIN.

Great or small?   225

SIR BOUNTEOUS.

At once I have drawn chain, jewel, watch, and all!

PENITENT.

By my faith, you have a fortunate hand, sir.

HAREBRAIN.

Nay, all to come at once.

MAWWORM.

A vengeance of this foolery!

213. How] *Q1* (*corr.*); Home *Q1*
(*uncorr.*).
215. watch'd] *Q1*; watch *Q2*.
220. german] *Q1* (*corr.*); Garman
Q1 (*uncorr.*).

223. or] *Q1*; or else *Q2*.
224. prize . . . prize] *Dyce*; peece . . .
peece *Q1–2*.
229. of] *Q1*; on *Q2*.

---

224. *prize*] See textual note. For the reverse of the misreading, cf. *No Wit,
No Help Like a Woman's*, I.ii.49, where the octavo reads "It was some price of
Land or money," and the emendation is "some piece."

FOLLYWIT.

 Have I 'scap'd the constable to be brought in by the watch? 230

COURTESAN.

 Oh destiny! Have I married a thief, mother?

MOTHER.

 Comfort thyself; thou art beforehand with him, daughter.

SIR BOUNTEOUS.

 Why son, why gentlemen, how long have you been my
Lord Owemuch his servants, i' faith?

FOLLYWIT.

 Faith, grandsire, shall I be true to you?   235

SIR BOUNTEOUS.

 I think 'tis time; thou'st been a thief already.

FOLLYWIT.

 I, knowing the day of your feast and the natural inclination
you have to pleasure and pastime, presum'd upon your
 patience for a jest as well to prolong your days as—

SIR BOUNTEOUS.

 Whoop! Why, then you took my chain along with you to 240
prolong my days, did you?

FOLLYWIT.

 Not so neither, sir; and that you may be seriously assured
of my hereafter stableness of life, I have took another course.

SIR BOUNTEOUS.

 What?

FOLLYWIT.

 Took a wife.   245

SIR BOUNTEOUS.

 A wife? 'Stoot, what is she for a fool would marry thee, a
madman? When was the wedding kept in Bedlam?

FOLLYWIT.

 She's both a gentlewoman and a virgin.

SIR BOUNTEOUS.

 Stop there, stop there; would I might see her!

FOLLYWIT.

 You have your wish; she's here.   250

235. shall I] *Q1*; I shall *Q2*.

---

246. *what . . . fool*] what kind of fool is she?

SIR BOUNTEOUS.

Ah, ha, ha, ha! This makes amends for all.

FOLLYWIT.

How now?

MAWWORM.

Captain, do you hear? Is she your wife in earnest?

FOLLYWIT.

How then?

MAWWORM.

Nothing but pity you, sir.   255

SIR BOUNTEOUS.

Speak, son, is't true?

Can you gull us, and let a quean gull you?

FOLLYWIT.

Ha!

COURTESAN.

What I have been is past; be that forgiven,

And have a soul true both to thee and heaven.   260

FOLLYWIT.

Is't come about? Tricks are repaid, I see.

SIR BOUNTEOUS.

The best is, sirrah, you pledge none but me;

And since I drink the top, take her; and hark,

I spice the bottom with a thousand mark.

FOLLYWIT.

By my troth, she is as good a cup of nectar as any bachelor 265

needs to sip at.

Tut, give me gold, it makes amends for vice;

Maids without coin are caudles without spice.

SIR BOUNTEOUS.

Come, gentlemen, to th' feast, let not time waste;

We have pleas'd our ear, now let us please our taste.   270

Who lives by cunning, mark it, his fate's cast;

When he has gull'd all, then is himself the last.

FINIS

272.] *Q2 adds* Exeunt.
272.1. FINIS] *not in some copies of*
Q1. Q2 adds: The end of the fifth
and last Act: marching over the
Stage hand in hand.

Appendix

Chronology

Approximate years are indicated by *, occurrences in doubt by (?).

Political and Literary Events	Life and Major Works of Middleton

1558
Accession of Queen Elizabeth.
Robert Greene born.
Thomas Kyd born.

1560
George Chapman born.

1561
Francis Bacon born.

1564
Shakespeare born.
Christopher Marlowe born.

1570
Thomas Heywood born.*

1572
Thomas Dekker born.*
John Donne born.
Massacre of St. Bartholomew's Day.

1573
Ben Jonson born.*

1576
The Theatre, the first permanent public theater in London, established by James Burbage.
John Marston born.

1577
The Curtain theater opened.
Holinshed's *Chronicles of England, Scotland and Ireland*.
Drake begins circumnavigation of the earth; completed 1580.

1578
John Lyly's *Euphues: The Anatomy of Wit*.

1579
John Fletcher born.
Sir Thomas North's translation of Plutarch's *Lives*.

1580

Baptized at St. Lawrence in the Old Jewry, London, April 18.

1583
Philip Massinger born.

1584
Francis Beaumont born.*

1586
Death of Sir Philip Sidney.
John Ford born.

1587
The Rose theater opened by Henslowe.
Marlowe's *TAMBURLAINE*, Part I.*
Execution of Mary, Queen of Scots.
Drake raids Cadiz.

1588
Defeat of the Spanish Armada.
Marlowe's *TAMBURLAINE*, Part II.*

1589
Greene's *FRIAR BACON AND FRIAR BUNGAY.*
Marlowe's *THE JEW OF MALTA.*
Kyd's *THE SPANISH TRAGEDY.*

1590
Spenser's *Faerie Queene* (Books I–III) published.
Sidney's *Arcadia* published.
Shakespeare's *HENRY VI*, Parts I–III,* *TITUS ANDRONICUS.*

1591
Shakespeare's *RICHARD III.*

1592
Marlowe's *DOCTOR FAUSTUS* and *EDWARD II.*
Shakespeare's *TAMING OF THE SHREW* and *THE COMEDY OF ERRORS.*
Death of Greene.

1593

Shakespeare's *LOVE'S LABOR'S LOST,** Venus and Adonis* published.
Death of Marlowe.
Theaters closed on account of plague.

1594

Shakespeare's *TWO GENTLEMEN OF VERONA;** The Rape of Lucrece* published.
Shakespeare's company becomes Lord Chamberlain's Men.
James Shirley born.*
Death of Kyd.

1595

The Swan theater built.
Sidney's *Defense of Poesy* published.
Shakespeare's *ROMEO AND JULIET,** A MIDSUMMER NIGHT'S DREAM,** RICHARD II.**
Raleigh's first expedition to Guiana.

1596

Spenser's *Faerie Queene* (Books IV–VI) published.
Shakespeare's *MERCHANT OF VENICE,** KING JOHN.**

1597

Bacon's *Essays* (first edition).
Shakespeare's *HENRY IV*, Part I.*

The Wisdom of Solomon Paraphrased (poem).

1598

Demolition of The Theatre.
Shakespeare's *MUCH ADO ABOUT NOTHING,** HENRY IV*, Part II.*
Jonson's *EVERY MAN IN HIS HUMOR* (first version).
Seven books of Chapman's translation of Homer's *Iliad* published.

Matriculated at Queen's College, Oxford, April 9.

1599

The Paul's Boys reopen their theater.
The Globe theater opened.
Shakespeare's *AS YOU LIKE IT,** HENRY V, JULIUS CAESAR.**
Marston's *ANTONIO AND MELLIDA,** Parts I and II.
Dekker's *THE SHOEMAKERS' HOLIDAY.**

Micro-Cynicon: Six Snarling Satires (poems).

Death of Spenser.

1600

Shakespeare's *TWELFTH NIGHT.*
The Fortune theater built by Alleyn.
The Children of the Chapel begin to play at the Blackfriars.

The Ghost of Lucrece (poem).

1601

Shakespeare's *HAMLET,** *MERRY WIVES OF WINDSOR.**
Insurrection and execution of the Earl of Essex.
Jonson's *POETASTER* (ridiculing Marston).

1602

Shakespeare's *TROILUS AND CRESSIDA.**

Married to Mary, or Magdalen, Marbeck.*
CAESAR'S FALL, with Dekker, Drayton, Munday, Webster (lost, Admiral's Men); *THE CHESTER TRAGEDY, OR RANDALL EARL OF CHESTER* (lost, Admiral's Men); *THE FAMILY OF LOVE** (Admiral's [?]). *BLURT MASTER CONSTABLE* (Paul's Boys).
December 14, receives five shillings for a prologue and epilogue for a court performance of *FRIAR BACON AND FRIAR BUNGAY.*

1603

Death of Queen Elizabeth; accession of James VI of Scotland as James I.
Florio's translation of Montaigne's *Essays* published.
Shakespeare's *ALL'S WELL THAT ENDS WELL.**
Heywood's *A WOMAN KILLED WITH KINDNESS.*
Marston's *THE MALCONTENT.**
Shakespeare's company becomes the King's Men.

THE PHOENIX* (Paul's Boys).
The True Narration of the Entertainment of His Royal Majesty from Edinburgh till London (pamphlet).

1604

Shakespeare's *MEASURE FOR MEASURE,** *OTHELLO.**
Marston's *THE FAWN.**
Chapman's *BUSSY D'AMBOIS.**

Son Edward born.*
The Ant and the Nightingale, or Father Hubburd's Tales; The Black Book (pamphlets).

THE HONEST WHORE, Part I, with Dekker (Prince Henry's Men); *THE PURITAN, OR THE WIDOW OF WATLING STREET*(?)* (Paul's Boys).

1605
Shakespeare's *KING LEAR.**
Marston's *THE DUTCH COURTESAN.**
Bacon's *Advancement of Learning* published.
The Gunpowder Plot.

MICHAELMAS TERM; A MAD WORLD, MY MASTERS; A TRICK TO CATCH THE OLD ONE (all acted by Paul's Boys).

1606
Shakespeare's *MACBETH.**
Jonson's *VOLPONE.**
Tourneur's *REVENGER'S TRAGEDY.**
The Red Bull theater built.
Death of John Lyly.

THE VIPER AND HER BROOD (lost).

1607
Shakespeare's *ANTONY AND CLEOPATRA.**
Beaumont's *KNIGHT OF THE BURNING PESTLE.**
Settlement of Jamestown, Virginia.

*YOUR FIVE GALLANTS** (Children of the Chapel).

1608
Shakespeare's *CORIOLANUS,**
*TIMON OF ATHENS,**
*PERICLES.**
Chapman's *CONSPIRACY AND TRAGEDY OF CHARLES, DUKE OF BYRON.**
Dekker's *Gull's Hornbook* published.
Richard Burbage leases Blackfriars Theatre for King's company.
John Milton born.

*THE ROARING GIRL,** with Dekker (Prince Henry's Men).

1609
Shakespeare's *CYMBELINE;** Sonnets published.
Jonson's *EPICOENE.*

Sir Robert Sherley's Entertainment in Cracovia (pamphlet).

1610
Jonson's *ALCHEMIST.*
Chapman's *REVENGE OF BUSSY D'AMBOIS.**
Richard Crashaw born.

1611
Authorized (King James) Version of the Bible published.

THE SECOND MAIDEN'S TRAGEDY (?) (King's Men); *A CHASTE*

Shakespeare's *THE WINTER'S TALE*,* *THE TEMPEST.** Beaumont and Fletcher's *A KING AND NO KING.* Tourneur's *ATHEIST'S TRAGEDY.** Chapman's translation of *Iliad* completed.

*MAID IN CHEAPSIDE** (Lady Elizabeth's Men); *WIT AT SEVERAL WEAPONS*,(?)* with Rowley (unknown company).

1612

Webster's *THE WHITE DEVIL.**

NO WIT, NO HELP LIKE A WOMAN'S (Lady Elizabeth's Men [?]).

1613

The Globe theater burned. Shakespeare's *HENRY VIII* (with Fletcher). Webster's *THE DUCHESS OF MALFI.** Sir Thomas Overbury murdered.

NEW RIVER ENTERTAINMENT September 29 (civic entertainment); *THE TRIUMPHS OF TRUTH*, October 29 (civic pageant).

1614

The Globe theater rebuilt. The Hope Theatre built. Jonson's *BARTHOLOMEW FAIR.*

THE MASQUE OF CUPID (lost, Merchant Tailors Hall).

1615

*THE WITCH** (King's Men); *MORE DISSEMBLERS BESIDES WOMEN** (King's Men).

1616

Publication of Folio edition of Jonson's *Works*. Chapman's *Whole Works of Homer*. Death of Shakespeare. Death of Beaumont.

THE WIDOW (?)* (King's Men); *HENGIST, KING OF KENT** (King's Men); *THE NICE VALOR*,(?)* with Fletcher (King's Men). *CIVITATIS AMOR* (civic pageant).

1617

THE TRIUMPHS OF HONOR AND INDUSTRY (civic pageant). *A FAIR QUARREL*, with Rowley (Prince Charles's Men).

1618

Outbreak of Thirty Years War. Execution of Raleigh.

THE OLD LAW,* with Rowley and Massinger (King's Men [?]). *The Peacemaker* (pamphlet).

1619

THE INNER TEMPLE MASQUE, OR MASQUE OF HEROES; THE WORLD TOSSED AT TENNIS,

with Rowley (Prince Charles's Men).
THE TRIUMPHS OF LOVE AND ANTIQUITY, October 29 (civic pageant).
On the Death of Richard Burbage (elegy).

1620
Pilgrim Fathers land at Plymouth.

Appointed City Chronologer, September 6.
The Marriage of the Old and New Testament (?) (pamphlet).

1621
Robert Burton's *Anatomy of Melancholy* published.
Andrew Marvell born.

ANYTHING FOR A QUIET LIFE,*
with Webster (?) (King's Men);
WOMEN BEWARE WOMEN*
(King's Men [?]).
THE SUN IN ARIES, with Munday
(?) (civic pageant); *HONORABLE ENTERTAINMENTS* (civic entertainments).

1622
Henry Vaughan born.

THE CHANGELING, with Rowley
(Lady Elizabeth's Men).
AN INVENTION FOR THE LORD MAYOR (private entertainment);
THE TRIUMPHS OF HONOR AND VIRTUE (civic pageant).

1623
Publication of Folio edition of Shakespeare's *COMEDIES, HISTORIES, AND TRAGEDIES*.

THE SPANISH GYPSY, with Rowley (?) (Lady Elizabeth's Men).
THE TRIUMPHS OF INTEGRITY (civic pageant).

1624

A GAME AT CHESS (King's Men).

1625
Death of King James I; accession of Charles I.
Death of Fletcher.

1626
Death of Tourneur.
Death of Bacon.

THE TRIUMPHS OF HEALTH AND PROSPERITY (civic pageant).

1627

Buried July 4 at Newington Butts.

1628
Ford's *THE LOVER'S MEL-
ANCHOLY.*
Petition of Right.
Buckingham assassinated.

1631
Shirley's *THE TRAITOR.*
Death of Donne.
John Dryden born.

1632
Massinger's *THE CITY MADAM.**

1633
Donne's *Poems* published.
Death of George Herbert.

1634
Death of Chapman, Marston,
Webster.*
Publication of *THE TWO NOBLE
KINSMEN,* with title page ascrip-
tion to Shakespeare and Fletcher.
Milton's *Comus.*

1635
Sir Thomas Browne's *Religio Medici.*

1637
Death of Jonson.

1639
First Bishops' War.
Death of Carew.*

1640
Short Parliament.
Long Parliament impeaches Laud.
Death of Massinger, Burton.

1641
Irish rebel.
Death of Heywood.

1642
Charles I leaves London; Civil
War breaks out.
Shirley's *COURT SECRET.*
All theaters closed by Act of Parlia-
ment.

1643
Parliament swears to the Solemn
League and Covenant.

1645
Ordinance for New Model Army
enacted.

1646
End of First Civil War.

1647
Army occupies London.
Charles I forms alliance with Scots.
Publication of Folio edition of
Beaumont and Fletcher's
COMEDIES AND TRAGEDIES.